# Contents

# First Peoples

Focus on Contemporary Issues (FOCI) addresses the pressing problems, ideas and debates of the new millennium. Subjects are drawn from the arts, sciences and humanities, and are linked by the impact they have had or are having on contemporary culture. FOCI books are intended for an intelligent, alert audience with a general understanding of, and curiosity about, the intellectual debates shaping culture today. Instead of easing readers into a comfortable awareness of particular fields, these books are combative. They offer points of view, take sides and are written with passion.

SERIES EDITORS
Barrie Bullen and Peter Hamilton

# First Peoples

## Indigenous Cultures and their Futures

JEFFREY SISSONS

REAKTION BOOKS

Published by Reaktion Books Ltd
33 Great Sutton Street
London EC1V 0DX, UK

www.reaktionbooks.co.uk

First published 2005
Transferred to digital printing 2009

Series design by Libanus Press
Printed and bound by Chicago University Press

*British Library Cataloguing in Publishing Data*
Sissons, Jeffrey
   First peoples: indigenous cultures and their futures
   1. Indigenous peoples - Ethnic identity  2. Indigenous peoples - Cross-cultural studies
   3. Indigenous peoples - Attitudes
   I. Title
   305.8

ISBN 978 1 86189 241 6

# Indigenism

Even the briefest of surfs through the sea of Internet resources will leave you in no doubt that the revival of indigenous cultures constitutes a movement of global scope and significance. Try typing 'indigenous cultures' into your Google search engine, for example: last time I was presented with 86,200 results that linked me to a mind-boggling range of cultural issues and hundreds of indigenous cultures. Top of my list was NativeWeb, one of the better non-profit sites, offering resource material on more than 300 different indigenous 'nations' or 'first peoples'. Most of its linked sites had been put up by indigenous people, for indigenous people, in order to share information on culture, history and politics. There were sites that provided news items and information on upcoming events, sites that were focused on international human rights and the environment, and sites that marketed indigenous art, music, film and tourism.

Quite apart from their Internet presence, the growth in indigenous film and tourism over the last decade is, in itself, further evidence of the increasingly global significance of indigineity. Films such as *Whale Rider*, based on a book by Maori writer Witi Ihimaera and set in a small Maori community, and *Rabbit-proof Fence*, describing the traumatic separation of Aboriginal children from their families, have been internationally acclaimed and viewed by millions of people. Many documentary films, less well known but arguably more indigenous, have been honoured at international festivals: Catherine Martin's documentaries on her Mi'kmaq people of Canada, for example, have won international awards and contributed to the revival of her people's cultural heritage. Indigenous cultural heritages have also become economic resources through the growth of eco-tourism and ethno-tourism. It is now possible for tourists from anywhere in the world to visit Kuna Indian communities in Panama, participate in Canadian First Nation dances, take kayak tours in the Arctic Nunavut, stay in a Maori home or spend a week in an indigenous village in the Amazon rainforest.

But there is a paradox in this globalizing of indigeneity: the concerns of most indigenous people remain deeply local and rooted in particular colonial struggles. The cultural politics of indigeneity continues to exert its greatest force in relation to the imagination of post-settler nationhood and the legitimacy of post-settler states. The increasingly global reach of indigeneity reflects not so much a transcendence of these particular national struggles as their spilling over into a wider political arena and global market-place. National issues such as indigenous education, indigenous authenticity, land rights and indigenous self-determination – issues that I address in this book – remain the most urgent ones for indigenous leaders, even when they seek greater recognition through international forums.

The greater audibility of an unmediated indigenous voice in the contemporary world represents a radical shift in the representation of first peoples, both within and beyond post-settler states. During most of the twentieth century indigenous images were treated as the common property of post-settler nations, freely available for use as symbols in the construction of nationhood. Maori carvings in New Zealand, Aboriginal people with spears and boomerangs in Australia, totem poles in Canada and scalp-hunting, tepee-dwelling Indians in the United States all referenced pre-colonial pasts out of which distinctive post-settler nations had emerged. Narratives of settler nationhood routinely employed indigenous imagery to create romanticized pasts that had been transcended or succeeded. As Nicholas Thomas has put it, these narratives of succession repeatedly proclaimed, in a bewildering variety of texts and images, that 'future is to past as settlers are to savages'.[1] The reappropriation of indigenous images by first peoples has deeply unsettled these narratives of settler nationhood because what was represented as past has since become most visibly and unmistakenly present. More than this, indigenous people are using these images to articulate new futures: now future is to past as 'savages' are to settlers! The appropriation of indigeneity by settler-states was, it turns out, merely cultural borrowing.

But it is not only images that have had to be returned: cultural objects, children, land, the right to self-definition and sovereignty have all been, or are in the process of being, reclaimed from post-settler states. Consider, for example, the reappropriation of the meeting-house named Mataatua by the Ngati Awa, a New Zealand Maori tribe. This large, elaborately carved building was constructed in the early 1870s as part of a wider process of cementing alliances between neighbouring tribes in response to land confiscation and military oppression by settlers. Carvers from different tribes were invited to contribute internal side posts and weavers provided spectacular latticework panels to fill the spaces between the posts. Some five years after its completion, the building was 'borrowed' by the New Zealand government and exhibited at the Inter-Colonial Exhibition in Sydney as a symbol of national distinctiveness. National appropriations of indigenous images often also entail their transformation, and in this case the transformation was particularly dramatic: in the process of exhibiting the building as a national possession it was emptied of people and literally turned inside out; the carved posts and lattice panels were placed on the outside. They suffered significant weather damage as a consequence.

This meeting-house was a building of innovative design, but it was exhibited as 'traditional' and emblematic of a culture that was destined to disappear. It subsequently became, like so many items of contemporary indigenous culture, a museum object. After Sydney, this vibrant example of living art was shipped to London, where it was dismantled and stored in the cellars of the Victoria and Albert Museum. In 1924 the meeting-house was reconstructed as an example of primitive art and as a symbol of one of Britain's subject races for the British Empire Exhibition held at Wembley Park – George v and Queen Mary were photographed standing on the porch. It was returned to New Zealand in pieces the following year and rebuilt within the walls of the Dunedin Museum.

I first visited the Dunedin Museum soon after taking up a teaching position at Otago University in Dunedin. I had recently been studying the history of the Tuhoe tribe, neighbours of the Ngati Awa from whom Mataatua had been 'borrowed', and had been living in a carved meeting-house of similar design and proportions while conducting my research. I had attended dozens, if not hundreds, of meetings and events (*hui*) held in and around such buildings. To meet Mataatua unexpectedly, with its carvings of Tuhoe and Ngati Awa ancestors so obviously out of place and out of time within the walls of the museum, was therefore a moving, even shocking experience for me. But if the sight of Mataatua in this colonial context was disturbing to me, it must have been much more so to Ngati Awa leaders. In 1985 they wrote to the Museum and asked for it back: 'This is an ancestral house, the oldest Ngati Awa house still standing, and it contains within it our ancestors. The house and our ancestors are standing in a "foreign land" where they do not belong. It is time for them to come home.'[2]

I was subsequently invited to a meeting at the Museum to advise the Director on how he might respond to such a request. My suggestion that they should give it back and ask for assistance in building a replacement went down like a lead balloon with the staff members at the meeting. But by the mid-1980s Maori political voices, in chorus with others throughout the indigenous world, were insisting that post-settler states had to acknowledge and provide redress for colonial injustices or lose their legitimacy. In response, the New Zealand Government established a tribunal to investigate breaches of the Treaty of Waitangi, signed by Maori leaders and the British Crown in 1840, and it would soon enter into negotiations with tribal leaders over appropriate compensation for Treaty breaches. Ngati Awa were able to negotiate the return of their meeting-house in 1996 and in a Deed of Settlement, signed in 2002, the New Zealand Government has promised to contribute $1 million towards the costs of developing a new cultural complex that will have the meeting-house at its centre.

This appropriation, transformation and reappropriation of indigeneity – whether it be of objects, identity, children, land or sovereignty – only appears to be a circular process; in fact, it is linear, with each stage directed towards the future. Indigenous reappropriations represent futures redirected. Ngati Awa leaders, for example, have their eyes firmly focused on projects of tribal development in which Mataatua will play a very different role to that which it has previously played. It is likewise for the children educated in Ngati Awa's tribal university and for the land returned under the Deed of Settlement. Nowhere in the indigenous world are cultural reappropriations regarded as returns to the past; rather, they are always reimaginations of the future. This book is a reflection on such reimaginings and on the conditions within which they are taking place.

Indigeneity exerts its greatest moral and political force in post-settler states that claim to represent, fairly and legitimately, the descendants of both colonizers and colonized. In order to maintain an illusion of political legitimacy these post-settler states have been forced to recognize the prior occupation of colonized peoples, or first peoples, and the right of these peoples to maintain and develop their indigenous cultures. Post-settler nationhood and indigeneity are, therefore, inseparable; they are two sides of the same coin, literally so in some cases. The New Zealand 10 cent piece, for example, has an image of the Queen of Great Britain and Head of the Commonwealth on one side, representing the settler nation, and a carved Maori face, representing indigeneity, on the other. As if to emphasize the association of 'tails' with indigeneity, the images on the reverse sides of other coins are of native fauna. In Brazil, where indigenous peoples comprise less than 0.2 per cent of the total population, their images are, nonetheless, also invoked in such banal constructions of national identity. The 1,000 cruzeiro bill in the 1980s, for instance, showed a Karaja Indian couple on one side and Marshall Rondon, creator of the Indian Protection Service, on the other. Similar examples can be found on the coins and notes of almost all post-settler states. These heads and tails images of settler nationhood and indigeneity are mundane assertions of the inseparability of the two identities and of the subordinate status of the colonized native. They also assert the success of the colonial project in uniting colonizer and colonized within a single nation, within a single economy. It is as if, in the contemporary world of global capitalism, we are all united within the nation-as-economy through the circulation of the coins that carry our identities.

But for most first peoples the other side of indigeneity is not simply settler nationhood as an alternative identity; it is settler nationhood as a project and grim vision that has historically sought the elimination of indigenous identities. In relation to such projects, contemporary first peoples can view their cultures only as cultures of survival. This does not mean that we should regard these cultures as being any less contemporary or dynamic than settler cultures. Rather, they represent a particular form of modernity that is characterized by an affirmation and conscious re-appropriation of tradition in opposition to the modernity proclaimed by post-settler states. And if indigenous cultures are cultures of survival, then judged in terms of their own progressive rationales, all projects of settler nationhood were failures. Indigenous cultures are not disappearing. The indigenous world is as diverse now as it ever was and, despite pessimistic predictions that colonized cultures would be absorbed into the nirvana of a new international order, this diversity shows no sign of reducing. Rather than following well-worn paths towards a uniform modernity, first peoples are, as I have already noted, envisaging alternative futures and appropriating global resources for their own culturally specific ends.

For Inuit and Cree in the northern hemisphere, for Maori and Aboriginal Australians in the southern, and for more than a hundred distinct peoples in-between, indigeneity has become more than heritage; like settler nationhood, it too is now a project. It is now clear that the numerous cultural renaissances that occurred throughout the indigenous world in the second half of the twentieth century were more than brief or passing events. Instead, their momentum has been maintained into the new millennium, while the challenges they pose to settler states and their bureaucracies have become increasingly urgent. Those who interpreted indigenous cultural 'revivals' as simply unconventional strategies in the pursuit of conventional economic and political objectives were wrong. What they failed to recognize was that the cultural objectives were radically distinct ends in themselves. True, the economic and political issues addressed by indigenous groups were and are depressingly similar – racism, loss of land and other resources, child abductions, inappropriate and inadequate health and education services, marginalization – but indigenous cultural solutions have been characterized by enormous diversity.

First peoples define themselves in terms of their cultural struggles against foreign cultural forces. Their cultures are those of prior occupation that are rooted in particular landscapes and histories. By contrast, the colonial cultures they struggle against originate over the horizon, and if they no longer cling precariously to the surfaces of their new land this is at least partly because their relationship to it has been mediated by indigenous thought and traditions. Indigenous place names have been retained in all post-settler states, for example, since to erase them completely from the territorial slate would have been to proclaim complete conquest, profoundly contradicting the settlers' self-understanding of their colonial project. Naming and renaming the land was, for the colonist, a civilizing process. For colonized peoples, however, it symbolized invasion and for this reason reassertions of indigenous place names have been fundamental to indigenous politics in many countries – North America became 'Turtle Island', New Zealand became 'Aotearoa'.

But indigenous identities have not arisen solely out of opposition with settler cultures. They have also been forged through alliances between indigenous peoples at international forums such as the UN Working Group on Indigenous Populations and in many other, less formal settings. Formal and informal alliances between indigenous peoples from different settler states highlight not only their shared history, but also their common objectives in achieving greater cultural autonomy within settler and post-settler states. Indigenous cultures and post-settler nations represent two sides of the same modernity – while the international movement of state politics appears to be towards greater uniformity, the indigenous world is moving in the opposite direction, defending and increasing its political and cultural diversity. This double movement is an expression of the increasingly contradictory nature of global politics in the twenty-first century.

In thousands of small indigenous communities people are increasingly being hooked into the globalized money economy, but this does not necessarily mean the erosion of local cultures – quite the opposite in many cases. The Yupik villagers of Togiak (in Bristol Bay, Alaska), for example, have purchased five aircraft to extend their subsistence caribou-hunting range; these are in addition to all-terrain four-wheel-drive vehicles, rifles and powered fishing vessels.[3] They, like many indigenous communities around the world, are using the proceeds that derive from participation in the global economy in order to reproduce their indigenous cultural orders. And we can extend this observation to individuals within these communities; for many, the greater their success in the money economy, the greater their participation in the indigenous culture. Even where this is not the case, distinctive indigenous values and interests usually underpin new forms of participation in national and global economies.

Cultural reproduction in new historical and global contexts is also cultural change. This must be so because, while the symbols and practices that constitute the outward expressions of indigenous culture often have ancient precedents, their meanings are always contemporary and changing. The meanings attributed by indigenous peoples to their art and material culture held by settler museums or by museums at the centres of empire may not always be those of their ancestors but they remain distinctively theirs and, as such, they are often radically different from the meanings attributed by national museums. A similar change overtakes local customs and knowledge recorded in publications by outsiders and indigenous scholars of an earlier period; when re-appropriated these indigenous possessions become charged with renewed significance within alternative cultural frames. Contemporary indigeneity is not simply about preserving traditions and meanings; it is also about their ownership and the ability to transform them in contexts where indigenous authenticity is policed and regulated by outsiders.

I define indigenous cultures, then, as cultures that have been transformed through the struggles of colonized peoples to resist and redirect projects of settler nationhood. I am well aware that for some political leaders, and perhaps most academic commentators, this definition is far too restrictive. What about tribal peoples in Africa and Asia who are not, or no longer, subject to oppressive projects of settler nationhood? Surely their cultures, too, are indigenous and worthy of greater political recognition. My response to such assertions is, first, to agree that there is an urgent need for greater understanding and international recognition of the threats posed to 'tribal' and subsistence-based cultures by national development programmes tied to the expansion of global capitalism. This is beyond question; nobody could reasonably deny that the Karen people of Burma and Thailand, the Orang Asli of Malaysia or the Maasai of Kenya are culturally endangered and that they suffer from oppressive state practices that deny them their cultural autonomy.

It is also important to recognize, however, that these cultural struggles of the Third World or developing world are in many ways quite distinct from those of the New World and the world of settler nations. Third World 'tribal' struggles are usually rooted in the cultural marginalization and oppression of less powerful indigenous peoples by more powerful ones. Indigeneity in such contexts is of little or no value as a marker of cultural or political distinctiveness. New World struggles, on the other hand, are rooted in the ongoing cultural marginalization and oppression of indigenous peoples by peoples whose cultures originated in Europe. In such contexts, indigeneity clearly references the other side of settler nationhood and serves as a powerful moral and political marker of cultural distinctiveness.

Failure to recognize this distinction at international forums has led to protracted disputes and a potentially serious loss of political direction in recent years. Over the last decade or so, as marginalized Third World peoples have joined the UN Working Group on Indigenous Populations, there has been a broadening of the definition of indigenous at the United Nations, so that it has now become widely equated with having subsistence economies and being close to 'Mother Earth'. This is eco-indigenism and it has two particularly unfortunate consequences. On the one hand, it primitivizes indigenous peoples living in settler states who have adopted urban lifestyles or it calls into question their authenticity; on the other hand, it opens up the possibility for almost any people with a subsistence-based culture to claim membership in international indigenous forums. Eco-indigenism entails a profound shift away from the original international meaning of 'indigenous' and I think there is a real danger that it will undermine the original international agenda of indigenous peoples in relation to settler nations.

I am certainly not alone in this assessment. Some indigenous leaders have become so concerned about the primitivist connotations of the term 'indigenous' that they have proposed abandoning it altogether. Members of the Ecuadorian contingent at the 2001 meeting of the UN Permanent Forum on Indigenous Issues declared, for example, that the term 'indigenous' was now an outdated way of representing otherness and that they should henceforth be known by their specific tribal names.[4] This was an understandable response by one of the most successful indigenous movements in Latin America to a shift in the political focus of the forum, away from indigenous democracy and self-determination within post-settler states and towards a more generalized defence of marginalized and endangered subsistence cultures. However, I do not think that the term 'indigenous' is in any sense outdated and nor do I think an international forum of distinctive tribal voices is a viable alternative. Instead, I argue in this book that we need to have a greater appreciation of indigenism as a distinctive form of identity politics within post-settler states. This distinctive political agenda deserves its own international forum.

Confusion has dogged international definitions of 'indigenous' since the 1980s when two authoritative meanings of the word were in circulation. The International Labour Organization's Convention 169, adopted in 1989, distinguished between 'tribal' and 'indigenous' peoples. Indigenous peoples were peoples in independent countries, who were regarded as indigenous:

on account of their descent from populations which inhabited the country, or a geographical region to which the country belongs, at the time of conquest or colonization or the establishment of present state boundaries and who, irrespective of their legal status, retain some or all of their own social, economic, cultural and political institutions.

In addition, the ILO definition stressed that 'self definition as indigenous or tribal shall be regarded as a fundamental criterion for determining the groups to which the provisions of this convention apply'.

Concurrent with this definition was another, proposed in 1986 by the UN Special Rapporteur, J. Matinez-Cobo. It also emphasized self-definition:

Indigenous communities, people, and nations are those which, having a historical continuity with pre-invasion and pre-colonial societies that developed on their territories, consider themselves distinct from other sectors of the societies now prevailing in those territories, or parts of them. They form at present non-dominant sectors of society and are determined to preserve, develop and transmit to future generations their ancestral territories, and their ethnic identity, as the basis of their continued existence as peoples, in accordance with their own cultural patterns, social institutions and legal systems.

Neither of these definitions distinguished clearly enough between New World indigenism and Third World eco-indigenism, and in their well-intentioned emphasis on self-definition they prepared the way for the conceptual and political confusion of the 1990s.

New World and Third World indigenisms are politically and conceptually grounded in different forms and phases of nationalism. Benedict Anderson, in his seminal work *Imagined Communities* (1983), locates the origins of nationalism in the New World of the eighteenth century. It was here that the idea of nationhood was created through a mix of progressive temporality, print capitalism and the frustrations of local officials who were ruled from Europe. Administrations in Venezuela, Mexico and Peru, for example, were headed by Spanish officials whose career paths included brief periods of service in the colonies. Local Creole officials, who could not go back 'home' to further their careers, developed a common sense of identity and purpose in opposing rule from afar; if they could not be Spanish then the Spanish could not be Venezuelan, or Peruvian or Mexican. A sense of distinctiveness from Europe developed strongly throughout North and South America, and this was reflected in the perspectives and content of local newspapers, of which 2,120 were published in the Americas between 1691 and 1820. Nationalist movements with progressive ideologies began in the Americas (the United States had declared its independence thirteen years before the French Revolution broke out) and notions of citizenship, national flags, national anthems and ideals of egalitarianism were all first developed in the New World.

This New World concept of the sovereign nation was, according to Anderson, modular. It was an idea that could be pirated by European elites in the nineteenth century. Old World nationalisms originated in such pirating and in the spectacular growth, in the late eighteenth and early nineteenth centuries, of printed works written in standardized national languages that were read by nationalizing bourgeoisies. Official nationalisms developed in response to populist movements. For example, the Russian court, whose language was French in the eighteenth century, nationalized itself through the adoption of the Russian language in the mid-nineteenth century. This new national language was then imposed on other developing nations within the empire – the Baltic countries became linguistic targets in 1887.

Finally, Anderson proposes, there was a 'last wave' of anti-colonial nationalism in European colonies. The conditions for this were created by the growth, in the colonies, of local intelligentsias who were not recognized as equals in the centres of colonial power. Their response was similar to that of the Creole officials, but now they had the models of the nineteenth-century European nations to follow. Developments in radio and mass rallies meant that colonial nationalists could bypass print in propagating their imagined communities to less literate populations. Colonialism had also created ready-made foundations in the census, map and museum: the census defined indigenous citizens, the map established internationally recognized boundaries and the museum supplied a cultural past.

But the history of nationhood was not simply the linear development of an idea, as Anderson implies; beyond Europe it was also the pursuit of two, quite distinct, types of political project. Within these two types of project the notion of indigeneity, or native belonging, had very different meanings. New World nationalism sought settler nationhood; it was a project pursued by the descendants of European settlers, through which they laid claim to a quasi-indigenous identity in relation to Europeans 'back home'. This meant an ambiguous imaginary relationship with the indigenous colonized; on the one hand, the relationship between colonizer and colonized constituted an obvious basis for claims of national distinctiveness, yet on the other hand the cultures of the indigenous colonized were regarded as obstacles in the path of achieving a nationhood that followed European models. Public displays of indigenous 'tradition' combined with policies of forced assimilation were, therefore, characteristic of this form of nationhood.

Anderson's 'last wave' of nationalism or, as I prefer, Third World nationalism, was a very different type of project entailing a different sense of indigeneity. Third World nationalisms that arose in opposition to European colonialism in Africa, Southeast Asia and the Middle East sought indigenous nationhood rather than settler nationhood. Here, settlers or their descendants did not constitute majorities in control of the state but ruled instead through alliances with sectors of the indigenous populations. Indigenous elites who belonged to these sectors and who, in many cases, were educated in Europe were supported in their nationalist projects by UN decolonization programmes in the period after the Second World War. Following formal independence, these indigenous elites embarked upon projects of 'modernization' and 'development' that targeted their 'backward' fellow citizens. Many of the world's most endangered cultures are tribal peoples under threat from such Third World nationalisms tied to globally funded 'development'. Forced assimilation, relocation, environmental destruction and ethnocide are all too frequently among the outcomes for these tribal peoples.

The political history of contemporary international indigenism reflects my distinction between settler and Third World nationalism. The earliest attempts at building an international indigenous movement grew out of the recognition, by leaders of colonized first peoples in North America, South America, Australia and New Zealand, of their common experiences in relation to settler nationhood. George Manuel, a member of Canada's Shushwap tribe and President of the National Indian Brotherhood, visited New Zealand Maori and Australian Aboriginal leaders in 1971. Upon his return to Canada he wrote: 'I hope that the common history and shared values that we discovered in each other are only the seeds from which some kind of lasting framework can grow for a common alliance of Native peoples.'[5]

The following year, the National Indian Brotherhood endorsed Manuel's plan for an international conference of indigenous peoples. A preparatory meeting was held in Guyana, in 1974, attended by representatives from Canada, the United States, Australia, New Zealand, Colombia and Guyana, as well as Norway, Finland, Sweden and Denmark. This meeting came up with an initial definition of 'indigenous' that stressed prior occupation and lack of control over the national government – no reference was made to minority status, tribal identity or closeness to nature:

'The term indigenous people refers to people living in countries which have a population composed of differing ethnic or racial groups, who are descendants of the earliest populations living in the area and who do not control the national government of the countries within which they live.'[6]

The stress on prior occupation and lack of governmental control was a reflection of what was to become the principal focus of the international indigenous movement – to challenge and ultimately limit the sovereignty of settler states. This objective was first clearly expressed at the conference to establish the World Council of Indigenous Peoples, hosted in Canada by a Nootka Indian band in 1975. Indigenous delegates from North and South America, Australia and New Zealand and Sami representatives from Norway and Sweden adopted a solemn declaration in which they asserted the continued existence of their peoples after centuries of colonial oppression and vowed they would 'control again [their] own destiny'.[7]

The establishment of the World Council of Indigenous Peoples helped pave the way for the establishment of the UN Working Group on Indigenous Populations (WGIP). Set up by the UN Economic and Social Council in 1982, the WGIP initially served largely as an international forum for addressing the concerns of indigenous peoples within settler states. In so doing it was furthering the political agenda of the World Council of Indigenous Peoples within the United Nations. As the membership expanded over the next twenty years, however, there was a broadening of focus to include issues associated with the political recognition and self-determination of marginalized cultural groups in Asian and African nations. Organizations from the Cordillera region in the Philippines and the Chittagong Hill Tracts in Bangladesh first attended WGIP meetings in 1984, and in 1987 delegations representing Ainu of Japan, Naga of India, Chin of Burma and Karen of Thailand joined the discussions. The first African group to be represented was the Maasai of Kenya in 1989. By the year 2000, the number of participants had grown from an original 30 to more than 1,000; around 90 indigenous organizations from settler states were joined by 40 organizations from Asia and 23 from Africa.[8]

As membership of the Working Group on Indigenous Populations expanded throughout the 1990s, the meaning of the term 'indigenous' became more confused and contested. On the one hand, Asian delegates questioned why European settlement should be considered a precondition for indigeneity and, on the other, a report was submitted that argued that most Asian, African and Russian delegations did not represent indigenous peoples at all – instead they represented 'minorities'.[9] In hindsight, the WGIP should perhaps have changed its name to the 'Working Group on Indigenous and Endangered Peoples' rather than persisting with attempts to stretch the meaning of 'indigenous' to fit its increasingly diverse membership. Had it done so, the specific issues raised by indigenism in relation to settler nationhood – issues that were core concerns for the original indigenous movement – may have retained a stronger distinctiveness in relation to eco-indigenism, which has since become the dominant discourse.

Eco-indigenism is a discourse that seeks to revalue primitivism and tribalism in relation to destructive western rationality and individualism. As such, it is not really about indigeneity in relation to settlement or colonization; it is, instead, about relative closeness to nature. Rather than a discourse of indigenism, it is perhaps better conceived of a discourse of eco-ethnicity in which ecological threat and destruction are 'ethnicized' and ethnic subordination is 'ecologized'.[10] Within the WGIP, eco-ethnic claims invariably invoke a distinctive cultural community living close to nature in a specific environment that is threatened with destruction. The community is portrayed as having an overriding moral responsibility to care for the threatened environment and to defend it against the destructive forces of western progress and global capitalism. Mining, logging, flooding owing to dams, biodiversity and intellectual property rights are issues of vital and urgent concern to many of the endangered cultures who participate in this discourse.

These issues are, of course, of equal concern to many indigenous peoples within settler states; mining has destroyed Aboriginal sacred sites in Australia, dams have flooded the lands of the James Bay Cree in Canada, logging and mining have wreaked environmental havoc in the Amazon rainforests. Global alliances between indigenous and endangered cultures in relation to such issues are, therefore, firmly grounded in shared experiences that are able to be articulated forcefully at forums such as the WGIP. However, widespread ecological destruction is not specifically a threat to indigeneity. Rather, it is more generally a growing threat to the cultural survival of a wide range of indigenous and endangered peoples who, in the most extreme cases, face cultural genocide. Publications such as *Cultural Survival Quarterly* and *Indigenous Affairs* serve a vital function in publicizing threats to tribal and subsistence cultures from mining, logging, dams and other forms of 'development' in all regions of the world, but because they do not make a distinction between endangered and indigenous cultures they have unwittingly perpetuated the confusion over the meaning of 'indigenous' that has developed within the WGIP.

This book is not about endangered cultures in general, nor is it about eco-ethnicity. Instead, I argue that indigenous cultures pose significant and specific challenges to settler and post-settler nationhood and that indigenism should therefore be understood as a form of global politics distinct from the more generalized projects of eco-ethnicity and cultural survival. Most indigenous cultures are also endangered and there are many concerns, especially those centred on the environment and property rights, that indigenous cultures share with most other endangered cultures. I have noted some of these above. Others include racism, the loss of heritage and traditional knowledge, and the loss of control over land and resources. But indigenism is more than resistance to cultural oppression and ecological threat. Indigenism in the twenty-first century will be defined by the ways in which it addresses specific issues that are grounded in relationships between indigenous cultures and post-settler nationhood. Foremost among these are: colonial and post-colonial regimes of oppressive authenticity; urban indigeneity; the education of indigenous children, indigenous citizenship and indigenous repossession. It is these concerns that are the focus of this book.

While it might appear that much of this book was written from an imaginary location somewhere in the middle of the Pacific Ocean, its perspective is sometimes that of a resident of Te Waimana, a rural Maori community in the North Island of New Zealand. Te Waimana will also be an imaginary location for most readers, but during the 1970s and early 1980s it was my home as I carried out research on traditional history and indigenous responses to colonialism. I have visited infrequently since then, most recently in order to attend meetings associated with a land claim for which I prepared a historical report. On a recent visit to the valley I noticed a painted wooden sign, nailed to a fence post, that read: 'You Are Entering the Territory of the Independent Tuhoe Nation'. The sign announces the political vision of some activist members of the Tuhoe tribe and reminds local leaders of what is at stake in current negotiations with the government over land rights. My understanding of the issues raised in this book is strongly coloured by such first-hand experiences and by what I have learned in conversation with Te Waimana elders.

In the early nineteenth century Te Waimana was a relatively prosperous community of around 150 people. They grew sweet potatoes, trapped eels, hunted birds and exchanged their forest foods for a variety of seafoods supplied by relatives living some 20 kilometres away on the coast. Later, when European traders arrived, people exchanged flax for guns and tools. In the mid-nineteenth century the New Zealand

Government confiscated all the land between Te Waimana and the sea and repeatedly attacked the inland communities, burning their houses, destroying their crops and driving people further inland into the dense forest. Military settlers were placed on the confiscated land and a Native Land Court was established to individualize the ownership of land that remained in Maori hands. As a direct consequence of the imposition of the Land Court, traditional leaders lost the ability to manage their land collectively in the interests of the whole community. Land became fragmented into smaller and smaller sections, many of which were sold because they were uneconomic. Those that were retained were farmed by a dozen or so families while most of the population survived as shearers and rural labourers, supplementing their income with hunting and gathering seafood.

Introduced diseases, including mumps, measles, whooping cough and typhoid, took a heavy toll in the early twentieth century and, in the absence of medical services, faith-healers worked to combat what appeared to be a rising tide of evil. The most prominent of these healers in Te Waimana was a man named Rua Kenana, who announced in 1906 that he was the New Messiah chosen by God to lead his people out of captivity. During a particularly severe typhoid epidemic Te Waimana parents took their children out of the government's Native School and followed Rua inland to build a new 'city of God'. The school had not only become physically dangerous in that it encouraged the rapid spread of infectious diseases, but it was also culturally dangerous in that it was undermining relations between children and their elders. A few years later Rua reached an agreement with leaders of the Presbyterian Church whereby he would keep the adults and the Church would have the children. Unlike the teachers at the Native Schools, the Presbyterian teachers learned to speak Maori and became part of the community.

Rua died in 1937 but his political and spiritual legacies remain. So too does the legacy of the Native Land Court. Te Waimana today is an impoverished valley in which only a few Tuhoe families are able to make a living from their land as dairy farmers. Land ownership retains a largely symbolic significance in that it underpins kin-group membership and a person's status as *tangata whenua* (someone who belongs to the land). However, most of the hundreds of families who belong to Te Waimana no longer live there – they live in New Zealand cities or in Australia, where their parents and grandparents moved in search of employment and a better life. Sometimes these urban dwellers return to one of twelve *marae* (ceremonial courts, each with a meeting-house and dining hall), especially when there is a *tangi* (funeral wake) for a close relative or an unveiling of a headstone in the local cemetery. Sometimes they send their children 'back home' in the hope that they will gain a more secure sense of their Maori identity and avoid the problems associated with urban alienation. Too often this only transposes urban problems into a rural setting – Te Waimana was recently divided into two gang territories, claimed by Black Power and the Mongrel Mob.

But Te Waimana remains a cultural wellspring and, along with neighbouring communities, a focus of tribal aspirations concerning economic development and self-determination. State-funded schools that teach in the Maori language have been established locally and there is also, nearby, a Maori University. Local leaders are participating in tribunal hearings that should result in compensation payments of tens of millions of dollars from the government for past land confiscations and other treaty breaches. The indigenous people of Te Waimana envisage their future in many different ways and reaching agreement will be far from easy. How can they best provide for their children's cultural needs? Who are authentically Tuhoe and hence the legitimate beneficiaries of compensation payments? What does self-determination mean for a tribe whose members live mostly in cities? How can they best develop urban-rural linkages? These are the sorts of questions with which this book is concerned and, as we shall see, they are by no means unique to Te Waimana.

One of the founding beliefs of settler nationhood was the assumption that indigenous cultures were less advanced than those of settlers; settlement was civilization. Civilization implied the disappearance of indigenous cultures, either through a 'natural' dying out of indigenous peoples or through their absorption by the new culture. In this ideological context official distinctions between authentic and inauthentic natives came to serve a number of ends associated with the management of indigenous peoples and the measurement of their disappearance. Settler-state regimes of oppressive authenticity were essentially about the granting of official recognition to a shrinking category of indigenous people who were deemed authentic and the denial of this recognition to an expanding category of others who were deemed inauthentic. In the next chapter I argue that the legacy of this oppressive authenticity in settler states constitutes a significant barrier to official and indigenous recognition of the dynamism of indigenous cultures and the increasing diversity of indigenous identities.

Perhaps the most serious omission from international debates on the future of indigenous cultures is inadequate recognition of the fact that most indigenous people now living in settler states are urban. The discourse of eco-ethnicity emphasizes the relationship between peoples and their natural environments – both are considered to be endangered simultaneously. In contrast, indigenism within settler nations is as much about the changing relationships between urban and rural communities and the emergence of indigenous urban cultures. These issues are discussed further in chapter Three, where it is also argued that the intersection of indigenism with class will have a significant influence on the development of indigenous cultures in the twenty-first century.

The project of settler nationhood was everywhere most crucially dependent upon the dispossession, by forces of the state, of indigenous land and children. Legislation enabling both forms of alienation – via confiscation, individualization of land ownership and compulsory schooling – was often enacted within the same decade. The loss of children from indigenous communities was often physical and symbolic; physical, in that children were abducted by state authorities or forced to attend distant boarding schools, and symbolic, in that children became culturally alienated from their families and home communities. The dispossession of children was intentionally aimed at limiting the inter-generational reproduction of indigenous cultures. In chapter Four I describe the devastating impact that this has had on indigenous cultures and consider some of the dilemmas faced by indigenous people as they seek to recover their children through the establishment of indigenous schools.

The international politics of ecological ethnicity does not forcefully address these issues of child recovery and increasing cultural diversity when it emphasizes, instead, the need to protect the autonomy and integrity of distinct tribal cultures. Similarly, on the question of indigenous citizenship rights, which I consider in chapter Five, the perspectives of indigenous peoples within settler nations are not as well represented as they might be. In the Declaration on the Rights of Indigenous Peoples drafted by the WGIP, for example, the increasing influence of eco-ethnicity is apparent in a bias towards self-determination for ecologically or tribally distinct groups. As one observer noted,

> Those peoples who are clearly observable as 'tribals' or 'primitives' (e.g. Yanomamis, Penan, Maasai, Nagas etc.) will be viewed as subjects of the rights of indigenous peoples. The fact is indisputable, however, that there are progressively fewer peoples who fall neatly into such categories.[11]

Indigenous citizenship is about rights for first peoples over and above those accorded to other, non-indigenous citizens. These do include self-determination, of course, but what this means for indigenous peoples who have become impoverished peasants or part of an urban proletariat within settler states is far from clear. What is certain is that the recognition of tribal autonomy will not adequately address questions of indigenous citizenship in the twenty-first century.

Indigenous cultures are not only indigenous, they are also *cultures*, and now very consciously so for indigenous peoples and settler states alike. Indigenism, like Edward Said's Orientalism, produces and reproduces cultural otherness. But indigenism differs from Orientalism in that indigenous peoples within settler states are participants in the construction of their own otherness as self-identity. In relation to Brazil, Ramos notes,

> Indians are equally agents in the country's indigenist project, no matter how constrained their agency may be. Moreover, when Indians seize on the notion of 'culture', an artefact of Western thinking about the other, to further their cause for ethnic recognition and self-determination, they contribute significantly to the design of indigenism.[12]

But we should not be too quick to label 'culture' as a western concept. Cultural revival was, in fact, first conceived as a political project within settler states by indigenous leaders seeking to counter the cultural hegemony of settler nationalism. One of the earliest breaks with assimilation in favour of a distinctive indigenous path of cultural preservation was that made by the New Zealand Maori leader Sir Apirana Ngata in the late 1920s. Influenced by the American cultural anthropology of Franz Boas, Ngata proposed that *Maoritanga* or Maori culture could serve as a strong foundation for Maori economic development and should be officially encouraged for this reason. During the 1928 election campaign Ngata bravely articulated his new cultural vision to voters: 'I told my audience that we had reached the point where we could select what we required of the culture of the Pakeha [European New Zealanders] and maintain so much Maori culture as showed persistence in the new environment. It was a bold thing to enunciate.'[13]

Ngata was Minister of Native Affairs at the time and he would lose his post as a result of his views. He was in office long enough, however, to launch a cultural revival programme in rural Maori communities. This was based around the construction of carved meeting-houses, modelled on the likes of Mataatua, and the revival of nineteenth-century dance, song and oratory traditions. The momentum that Ngata built up for this programme ensured that *Maoritanga* would remain an alternative project to that of assimilation for the remainder of the twentieth century.

Ngata's cultural renaissance coincided with a greater recognition of indigenous cultures in the United States and Mexico. Under Franklin Roosevelt's presidency in the 1930s the Commissioner of Indian Affairs, John Collier, promoted a vision similar to that of Ngata. Measures such as the Indian Reorganization Act, passed by Congress in 1934, represented a rethinking of assimilation, or at least the means by which it would be achieved. Allowing for some Indian cultural distinctiveness in the short term might assist their assimilation in the longer term. At the same time, in Mexico, the progressive President Lázaro Cárdenas was reforming indigenous education and funding indigenous congresses. These reforms accorded greater recognition to Indian cultural distinctiveness, although the goal of ultimate assimilation remained unchanged.

Although the binary of indigenism has sanctioned indigenous cultural distinctiveness since the 1930s it has also limited it. First, it has often been seen as a temporary or transitional state of affairs. Second, it has tended to homogenize both indigenous and settler cultures. If indigenous cultures are imagined as unitary in their contrasts with settler cultures or settler nationhood, then indigenous cultural diversity can only be sanctioned within the limits imposed by these contrasting relations. If cultural difference between indigenous peoples threatens the status of indigeneity within particular settler states, then cultural sharing between indigenous peoples and the descendants of settlers poses an equal threat. During the 1930s leaders such as Ngata had to struggle to find a way of partitioning off hybridity so that it would not infect the fundamental relationship between two cultures. Things have become much more complex since. We now need to ask how much cultural hybridity can there be before the binary of indigenism disintegrates under the weight of excessive diversity? Is post-indigenism conceivable? Would it simply be assimilation under a new name? I discuss post-indigenism and its relationship to post-colonialism in the concluding chapter.

This book is not a survey. It would be impossible in a book this size – in a book any size – to do justice to the full diversity of indigenous cultures within contemporary post-settler states. Instead, this book is an argument about the future of indigeneity, an essay about some crucial issues that confront first peoples and their cultures in the early twenty-first century. In order to make my case I have drawn upon a wide range of examples, but not every post-settler state is represented. The United States, Canada, Australia, New Zealand, Mexico and Brazil feature promi- nently, and I also make reference to Panama, Bolivia, Colombia and Peru. I often refer in general terms to the first peoples of these states, but I also include more in-depth discussions of Navajo, Cherokee, Oneida and Native Hawai'ians in the United States, Inuit and Kwakiutl in Canada, Kayapo in Brazil, Maya of Chiapas in Mexico, Tuhoe, Ngati Awa and Ngai Tahu in New Zealand, and Yawur and Cape York people in Australia. There are, of course, many other indigenous cultures that I could have chosen to focus on, but I do not think alternative examples would have signifi- cantly altered my main arguments. This book is intended to provoke and challenge rather than advocate on behalf of first peoples. But this does not mean it is politically neutral. I make no apologies for the fact that in relat- ing the histories of dispossession suffered by first peoples I have frequently found it impossible to retrain myself from advocacy and expressions of moral outrage.

As an anthropologist and as a human being living in a multi-cultural society I am reminded, almost daily, of the fact that no culture is clearly bounded in relation to any other. Indeed, the very notion of a world divided up into entirely discrete cultures, some of which are indigenous and some of which are not, strikes me as an absurdity. Within any post-settler state there is a huge amount of cultural sharing going on, providing fertile ground for cultural invention. But to recognize that cultures are not discrete – that they overlap and have fuzzy edges – is not to say that they are without cores or centres. *Cultures have hearts.*

At the heart of all indigenous cultures are relations between kin that differ profoundly from the ways that kin relations are practised and understood in settler cultures. Kinship in most indigenous cultures includes an ongoing relationship with the land and natural environment, for example, an understanding that is entirely absent from settler cultures that originated in Europe. This indigenous understanding of kinship extends from cosmology to political and economic life and provides a foundation for cultural resistance to the rational operation of state power within post-settler states. A fellow anthropologist, Marshall Sahlins, has recently argued that his discipline needs to be as concerned with the resistance of culture as it is currently with cultures of resistance. Kinship is the place to start if we are to understand indigenous cultural resistance.

At the heart of settler cultures is a gendered and rugged individualism that views land and the natural world as needing to be brought under control. This individualistic and adversarial relationship with the environment extends from western cosmology to political and economic life as surely as does kinship for indigenous cultures, providing a foundation for the operation of state power and bureaucratic rationality within post-settler states. Kinship cosmologies and kin-based polities do not sit easily with systems based on bureaucratic rationality. Bureaucratic reason is best suited to the management of secular individuals separated from their kin and the associated obligations that these relations entail; in bureaucratic cosmologies the head rules the heart – generosity, love, hatred and honour have no recognized place.

I am talking in huge generalities here, but that is the point: I think it is possible to identify different cultural centres within post-settler states and at the same time recognize that there is an enormous amount of cultural sharing and diversity around the edges. The indigenous cultures that I write about in this book are all internally diverse and, to varying degrees, share languages, ideas and values with settler cultures. Differences between the daily lives of urban and rural indigenous people can be as great as differences between the lives of indigenous people and others living within the post-settler state. Intermarriage between settlers and indigenous people does not automatically lead to a merging of their cultures – often the children of such marriages learn mainly the culture of one parent only. However, a high degree of intermarriage has certainly contributed to a greater diversity within some indigenous cultures.

Culture is infectious. Some anthropologists have recently advocated taking an epidemiological approach to culture, investigating factors that influence its spread – low and high resistance, mutation, levels of interaction between groups, for example. While I think this smacks a little too strongly of biology, there is no doubt that globalized images originating in centres of global power 'infect' us all – stimulating us, seducing us and appalling us. Indigenous people are no less engaged by such images than anyone else, although the images and ideas that they choose to adopt and adapt may be quite different from those chosen by their fellow citizens. Hip-hop and Rastafarianism are more popular with working-class Maori than the latest New York fashions, for example. Rather than blurring differences between indigenous cultures and others within a post-settler state, globalization may, therefore, enhance indigenous distinctiveness. Globalization is always also localization, and localization is sometimes indigenization.

Indigenism, as a distinctive form of identity politics within post-settler states, will be an enduring phenomenon despite globalization. The pasts and futures of nations of the New World will continue to be imagined within and against this politics. The challenge for first peoples is to ensure that post-settler nations become post-colonial nations within which their past and future identities are secure.

# CHAPTER TWO

# Oppressive Authenticity

Why should first peoples be expected to have authentic identities while settlers and their descendants remain largely untroubled by their own ill-defined cultural characteristics? Why should indigeneity as opposed to migration be especially associated with cultural purity? At least part of the answer must lie in earlier racial understandings of the relationships between colonizers and colonized and between the colonized and their natural environments; indigenous authenticity is racism and primitivism in disguise. For nineteenth-century Europeans the human species consisted of different races inhabiting different environments and this explained differences in appearance and thought. We now divide humanity into different cultures instead, and culture, not race, is said to explain differences in thought. But the earlier racial thinking persists in the shadow of the new culturalism. You might say that the logic of dividing colonized others into distinct races has been reproduced in the logic of their division into distinct cultures, but this does not mean that it has also been completely displaced. As disciples of the philosopher Derrida would put it, racism now exists as a trace, a ghostly presence that haunts culturalist thought. If indigenous peoples are to be recognized as culturally authentic they are often expected to look and sound indigenous too.

Listen, for example, to the following conversation overheard by an Amazonian Indian on a train in Brazil:

> See that young man? He looks Indian, said lady A.
>
> Yes he does. But I'm not sure. Haven't you noticed he is wearing jeans? He can't be an Indian and wear Whiteman's clothes. I don't think he is a real Indian, contested lady B.
>
> Yah, maybe. But can't you see his hair? Straight hair. Only Indians have hair like that. Yes, I think he's an Indian, Lady A said, defending me . . . his cheeks jut out. Only Indians have a face like that. No he can't deny it. He can only be an Indian, and a pure one it seems . . .[1]

Apparently, the ladies on the train were quite unconcerned about the possibility that they might be overheard. The person who sat in front of them was an ambiguous presence to be talked about rather than to – after all, they could simply have asked the man if he was Indian; he appeared to them as a mute form of otherness that refused easy categorization. For one of the women, the man's dress constituted a cultural façade that obscured a deeper biological purity. For the other, his contradictory appearance signified impurity and inauthenticity.

In her book *Purity and Danger*, the anthropologist Mary Douglas argued that impurity and danger are everywhere attributed to things, animals and people that are anomalous or ambiguous in terms of accepted categories. Dirt is matter out of place. Sticky stuff is neither liquid nor solid; it clings to us, threatening to dissolve the boundaries between us and the world. If penguins or kiwi had lived in the Near East they would probably have been among the abominations of Leviticus because they are flightless birds.[2] Indigenous racial impurity has been regarded as similarly threatening to the natural order and a cause for colonial and post-colonial concern.

Indigenous purity has been, and continues to be, of intense interest to settler and post-settler governments that require varying degrees of biological and cultural authenticity before granting political recognition and economic support to indigenous people. These requirements of authenticity can, in themselves, become oppressive. Oppressive authenticity operates primarily as a mechanism of exclusion; those who cannot be placed securely within one of two categories – 'native' or 'settler' – become people out of place. They do not properly belong in the official scheme of things; they are impure, inauthentic and too often become an excluded middle.[3] The operation of oppressive authenticity has been integral to the foundation of all settler nations and it continues to haunt the formation and implementation of their cultural policies. Included in the excluded middles of many post-settler states today are millions of indigenous people variously described as 'half-castes', 'mixed-bloods', 'urbanized', 'non-traditional' and 'westernized' – usually the majority of their indigenous citizens.

Oppressive authenticity requires that the distinctions between 'native' and 'settler' be continuously reproduced, although always in new guises. Racial and evolutionary categories continue to inform this process. Indigenous people are expected to be essentially 'other' and to manifest this otherness in natural and visible ways. To be *naturally* other is to remain part of the landscape, to be intimately linked to the ecology of the country like trees and rivers and animals. It is to be primitive, to live simply and close to nature. Urban indigeneity is, therefore, regarded as an anomalous condition for indigenous people. When indigenous people make new lives in towns and cities they become people out of place. This association of indigeneity with notions of idealized simplicity and ecological belonging recalls earlier evolutionary narratives in which racial groups were positioned hierarchically in terms of their levels of technological development. As I noted in the last chapter, the international discourse of eco-indigeneity reproduces this understanding in a more innocent guise.

Nineteenth-century Romanticism invoked images of indigenous purity and naturalness as nostalgic affirmations of the advance of European civilization. Now, the same images, digitally enhanced, are used by environmentalists as proof of its decadence and decline. For Romanticism, nature was a source of purity and goodness distinct from the works of rational 'man'; 'God made the country and man made the town' as the poet William Cowper put it. Nature, a mystical substitute for God, became the source of sublime inspiration and feelings. Indigenous people, who were viewed as part of nature, were also expected to be pure and good; those who were not had fallen from grace. Twenty-first century environmentalism draws upon this romantic view to sustain a discourse of planetary crisis. Indigenous peoples remain oppressed by expectations that they be pure and natural; those who do not conform to these western ideals are frequently condemned as contaminated, impure and inauthentic. All too easily it is assumed that 'ecologically inauthentic' indigenous cultures have 'sold out' to the west. Caught again in a binary not of their own making, 'ecologically inauthentic' indigenous people risk the same exclusion as that imposed on the racially inauthentic. And, of course, they are often the same people.

In this context, an ability to project eco-authenticity, especially through visual images such as body decoration, can bring much needed political support and substantial economic rewards. This has been most strikingly evident in Amazonian eco-politics, where authenticity is now routinely indexed through body paint, semi-nudity and colourful ornamentation. The Kayapo of central Brazil are widely acknowledged as the masters of the use of exotic body images to preserve self-determination and retain control over land. An early media-opportunity was the visit of a musician, Sting, to a Kayapo village in 1988. Reports of the visit in the world's media were invariably accompanied by images of people in body paint and/or men with large lip-discs. In *People* magazine, Sting was quoted as saying, 'It didn't take long for the varnish of civilization to leave us. After 48 hours, we were naked, covered with paint and fighting snakes.'[4] However,

Terrence Turner, an anthropologist who has worked with the Kayapo for many years, has recorded that when he arrived in 1962 most men had removed their lip-plugs and were wearing shorts and occasionally t-shirts in the village visited by Sting.

There is no doubt that deploying images of eco-authenticity has been an extremely successful strategy for the Kayapo, who, as a small group (about 4,000) and living in an extremely remote part of the world, relied on media exposure to protect them from unscrupulous logging, mining and dam-building interests backed by the Brazilian state. By their astute use of the world media and through strategic alliances with environmental organizations, Kayapo have halted the construction of the world's largest dam, prevented the dumping of radioactive waste on their land, asserted direct control over gold and timber operations, and won legal rights to territory about the size of Scotland.[5]

In the longer term, however, there may be a high price to be paid for conforming to western stereotypes of eco-authenticity. The problem with relying on the global media is that it is not always supportive of indigenous interests. A number of right-wing magazines have sought to 'expose' the Kayapo and other Indian groups as inauthentic by publishing 'before and after' photographs of Kayapo activists: photos of people in costume and out of costume – dressed in western clothing, driving cars and eating at restaurants. The politics of eco-authenticity can become a dangerous game when media interests and indigenous interests diverge.

Perhaps even more damaging are the hierarchies of eco-authenticity that may be created through differences in the abilities of indigenous peoples to conform to western ideals. In Colombia, for example, lowland Amazonian Indians are officially viewed as more authentic than Andean Indians, while the hunting and gathering Maku are regarded as more pure than their Tukanoan neighbours, who are horticulturalists. In Brazil, the Kayapo have established a standard of visual eco-authenticity that other groups have been forced to match in order to retain public and political support. For example, the Pataxo Indians on the Atlantic coast decided to adopt feather headdresses after their authenticity was publicly questioned by the leader of a congressional delegation. The Pataxo had been engaged in a struggle to defend their coastal lands and were besieged by some 3,000 armed settlers when the delegation visited them in the late 1980s. Talks broke down, however, and the leader of the congressional delegation subsequently declared that part of the problem was that the Pataxo were not real Indians. They were not authentic because they did not look authentic: 'Indians don't have beards or moustaches and body hair', he asserted.[6]

The politics of authenticity forces some people to become authentic by becoming inauthentic. The Pataxo have become more 'real', some would say hyper-real, since the onset of their coastal land dispute. Within Brazil there have also been pressures upon other indigenous groups, whose dress and appearance differ markedly from the Kayapo, to do likewise. Not to do so is to lose out in the national and international popularity stakes. For example, the Wari, another Brazilian people, have had less success than the Kayapo in attracting media attention because, rather than donning elaborate feather headdresses, they traditionally stick bits of white down onto oiled hair – a less appealing image for western audiences.

The operation of an oppressive eco-authenticity is most evident in Brazil and more widely in South America. However, it is also present, to some degree and in different forms, in all post-settler nations. Australian Aboriginal people must be able to demonstrate continuous traditional links with their land in order to have their rights and identities officially recognized. In New Zealand and Hawai'i the official recognition of spiritual connections with the land has been denied to urban residents and protestors. It is common for the organizers of indigenous land rights protests to be accused by their opponents of faking their eco-authenticity and inventing spiritual traditions.

In addition to being naturally other, indigenous people are expected to be visibly other. To be visibly other is, above all, to be phenotypically different. Hair, skin colour and facial features are assumed to index levels of 'genuine' racial, and by extension, cultural belonging. Ideally, there should also be no contradiction between these visible biological elements and cultural ones such as speech, dress and manner. Where these two dimensions of visible identity do contradict each other, as they did for the Indian on the train, then indigenous authenticity, and with it personal integrity, is thrown into question. And let there be no doubt: the *very question* of indigenous authenticity has deep roots within colonial racism. Official binaries and the excluded middles that they produce within settler and post-settler states are not only legacies of colonial invasion; they draw upon and are sustained by racist thought that continues to be obsessed with indigenous blood.

A whole mathematics of blood quantum was developed by colonial settlers in the United States, Australia, Canada and New Zealand as a pseudo-scientific foundation for indigenous exclusion. Blood that is not pure is, by definition, impure. The mathematics of blood quantum defined stages or degrees of this impurity in order to rationalize a host of oppressive measures from Aboriginal child abduction in Australia to massive land alienation in the United States. The legacy of this bloody classification continues to haunt indigenous people in these countries and throughout the post-settler world. Even where there have been efforts to address the effects of biological exclusion, as there have been recently in Canada, they have resulted only in its perpetuation under a new guise.

Between 1909 and 1969 it was official government policy in Australia to remove Aboriginal children, especially 'half-castes' and those with lighter skins, from their families to be brought up in 'white' society. This practice had begun in the nineteenth century and was given legal sanction through the ironically titled 'Aborigines Protection Act' of 1909. An amendment to this Act in 1915 enabled any Aboriginal child to be taken from his or her family without the family's consent and without a court order. Most children were raised in church or state institutions, while some were adopted or fostered by white parents. Many were physically and sexually abused and suffered rejection from the very society into which they were supposed to be assimilating. Parents were not told where their children had been taken and were unable to trace them. These children were described by Peter Read as 'the stolen generations'.[7] Between 10 and 30 per cent of all Aboriginal children were abducted and almost every Aboriginal family in Australia has been affected in some way by this deeply racist practice. After reading the harrowing reports of social devastation and human suffering we are left wondering how government officials and social welfare staff could have possibly justified the practice to themselves and the wider public.

Throughout most of the nineteenth century it was assumed that Aboriginal people, confined largely to mission stations and reserves outside white society, would quietly die out. By the 1880s, however, it was realized that their numbers were actually increasing and that a growing proportion of Aboriginal children had European fathers and/or grandfathers. Thus was born the popular European notion of a growing 'half-caste menace' threatening white identity and, with it, the policy of assimilation. The future of assimilation was under threat because, although these Aboriginal children had white fathers, they remained Aboriginal. The Victoria Act was passed in 1886 to deal with this intolerable situation; it did so by defining as 'non-Aboriginal' all Aboriginal people of mixed descent. These 'non-Aboriginal' Aboriginal people thus became an anomalous group that needed to be eliminated through assimilation into white society. The licensed abduction of children that followed was therefore understood by officials as a way of giving those children who did not properly belong within Aboriginal society a more secure place within the white nation. Of course, from an Aboriginal point of view these children *did* fully belong to their communities and their forced removal was widely experienced by all involved as an act of state terror.

Aboriginal child abduction was further legitimized by a strange pseudo-mathematics of biological authenticity.[8] When expressed as racial purity, Aboriginality was mathematically divisible: parents were halves; grandparents were quarters, and so on. A precise terminology was evolved to identify the different proportions of white admixture, and hence degrees of racial authenticity; on the path to assimilation 'full-bloods' became 'half-castes', 'half-castes' became 'quadroons', and 'quadroons' became 'octoroons'. Beyond 'octoroon' children were deemed to be officially white, that is, full members of the white Australian nation. A similar algebra was practised in North America and New Zealand. It is significant that white society was deemed able to absorb any amount of Aboriginal admixture and remain white, while any amount of European 'blood' rendered Aboriginal identity inauthentic[9] and thus a candidate for elimination through assimilation. As I have already noted, only indigenous people are expected to remain purely other; this is not required of the settler self.

In response to a public outcry over the revelations of Aboriginal child abduction by Peter Read and others, a national inquiry was initiated by the Human Rights and Equal Opportunity Commission. The Inquiry report,[10] tabled in the Federal Parliament in May 1997, concluded that the abductions were contrary to the UN convention on genocide that forbids the forcible transfer of children from one group to another with the intention of destroying the group. It recommended that records be opened up, the establishment of tracing services, compensation and apologies. All but one of the state governments has since apologized, as have many local governments, NGOs and church groups. However, the Federal government remains in deep denial and has refused to offer an apology; ministers have argued that the policy was well intentioned and that it did not cause deep distress. No doubt the Federal response can be partly explained by the fact that court action seeking compensation from the government is already under way.[11] But an additional constraint is the general inability of the government and a sizeable proportion of its constituency to accept the racist foundations of the Australian post-settler nation.

By not facing up to this indigenous challenge to Australian nation-hood the Federal government is actually increasing the burden and distress currently experienced by Aboriginal people resulting from child abductions. In addition to the emotional stress, it is likely that many members of the stolen generations will be unable to establish their rights to native title, since in order to do so they need to be able to demonstrate continuous traditional ties with their land and communities.

It cannot have been accidental that indigenous assimilation policies were launched in Australia and the United States at almost exactly the same time. A year after the passing of the 1886 Victoria Act in Australia, which also provided for the break-up of Aboriginal reserves, the Dawes Act was passed in the United States. More correctly known as the General Allotment Act 1887, this was designed to break up communally owned land through the assignment or allotment of blocks to individuals: heads of families received 160 acres; unmarried people over 18 years of age and orphans under 18 received 80 acres each; and others under 18 received 40 acres. Citizenship was conferred upon allottees and others who abandoned their tribes and adopted 'the habits of civilized life'.[12]

The most devastating provision of the Act was the clause permitting the government to purchase all the land that remained after blocks had been allotted to individuals – the so-called surplus land. The amount of land designated as 'surplus' was often much greater than the land that had been allotted. For example, the 2,000 Sisseton Indians of South Dakota, a branch of the Sioux tribe, were able to retain 300,000 acres through allotment, but this left approximately 600,000 acres in the surplus category, which was immediately made available for white settlement. By 1909 two-thirds of the allotted land had also been sold, leaving only 35,000 acres in the hands of the original allotment holders and 80,000 acres, cut up into smaller and smaller parcels, in the hands of their heirs. Between 1887 and 1934 the land held by Native Americans in the United States was legally reduced, through the provisions of the Dawes Act, from 138 million to 48 million acres.[13] It has been argued that this legislation was at least as destructive of indigenous societies as earlier military action.

A particularly pernicious consequence of the Dawes Act was the introduction of the notion of 'blood quantum' into American Indian policy. Only Native Americans living on reservations who could document one-half or more Indian 'blood' were eligible for allotments. Those who could not were simply excluded.[14] The inability of many indigenous Americans to document a sufficient amount of 'blood' greatly reduced the amount of land allotted to tribes and so increased the extent of the 'surplus lands'. Unlike the child abductions in Australia, which were directed at the assimilation of half-castes, the Dawes Act was directed at the assimilation of all Indians. Those with half Indian 'blood' or more became (however briefly) individualized owners, while those with less Indian 'blood', or those who were unable to document their blood quantum, became landless individualized labour.

The notion of blood quantum has since become central to the administration of the Bureau of Indian Affairs. In most states a blood quantum of a quarter, together with a Certificate Degree of Indian Blood (CDIB) that has been authenticated by a recognized tribe, is required in order to gain access to targeted services. Moreover, Indian nations have themselves imported the idea of blood quantum as a criterion for citizenship and access to resources and services. The Navajo require at least one-sixteenth 'Indian blood', while the Cherokee require some 'Indian blood' but have set no minimum level – degrees of Indian blood within the Cherokee nation vary from full blood to $1/_{2,048}$ blood.[15]

The state ideology of blood purity with respect to indigenous peoples has become a source of political tension within indigenous nations such as the Cherokee. By setting a restrictive blood quantum, some nations replicate the racist exclusion begun by the Federal government in the Dawes Act. But by following the Cherokee in not setting a minimum quantum, other, equally pressing political and economic issues are raised. Circe Sturm, in her wonderfully insightful book *Blood Politics*, has shown how racial understandings have become central to the construction of Cherokee identity partly as a result of the nation's unrestrictive blood quantum. Since the removal of the restrictions in the 1970s the Cherokee nation has more than quintupled in size, from less than 40,000 citizens in 1982 to currently more than 200,000.[16] But as it grows, the nation also becomes progressively 'whiter' and so vulnerable to a withdrawal of Federal recognition. As Sturm notes, 'even now, the federal government might reclassify most Cherokee citizens as non-Indians in order to save itself some money'.[17]

Within the Cherokee nation there is, understandably, greater support for a more restrictive blood quantum requirement among the more culturally conservative citizens with higher proportions of Indian blood. Many of these do not vote in Cherokee elections because they believe that the nation, as it is currently constituted, does not represent them or their interests. Most Cherokee, however, do not want a more restrictive blood quantum because it would exclude them from membership.[18] All are caught in an ideological trap not of their own making: to continue to base Cherokee identity on blood is to belong to an increasingly 'white' nation; but to de-racialize tribal identity (by replacing blood with residence criteria and an oath of allegiance, for example) is to lose Federal recognition and funding. Repressive biological authenticity is by no means restricted to the nineteenth and twentieth centuries.

Indigenous blood-policing has recently been extended to the creative arts in the United States following the signing into law of the Indian Arts and Crafts Act. The Act's intention is to protect Native Americans engaged in the arts and crafts market from non-Indians who might seek to market items that falsely suggest authentic Indian origins. But there is a catch. Indian artists and crafts producers are now required to prove their authenticity in order to continue their work and for many this creates practical, political and personal difficulties. The Act requires these people to be members of federally recognized tribes or to be certified by one of these tribes. Many have been unable to meet the varying blood quantum and descent requirements of tribes and so have been excluded from participation, as Indians, in the art market.

Others, such as the Cherokee artist Jimmie Durham, view this legislation as an extension of the racist Dawes Act in its equating of blood quantum with authenticity and have refused to be certified as Indian under its provisions.[19] Durham's refusal to have his authenticity bureaucratically defined quickly resulted in the cancellation of two exhibitions of his work in 1991. Durham considers himself to be an artist who happens to be Cherokee, resisting the particularization of his work as indigenous. Following the cancellation of these exhibitions, he produced a disclaimer that he posted at subsequent exhibitions:

> I hereby swear to the truth of the following statement: I am a full-blood contemporary artist, of the sub-groups (or clan) called sculptors. I am not an American Indian, nor have I ever seen or sworn loyalty to India. I am not a Native 'American', nor do I feel that 'America' has any right to either name me or un-name me. I have personally stated that I should be considered a mixed-blood: that is, I claim to be male but in fact only one of my parents is male.[20]

This delightful parody of blood-quantum-linked certification accords with the more general political message embodied in much of Durham's work. For example, *Self-Portrait*, produced in 1987, was a large two-dimensional figure that was dissected and labelled like a map, suggesting the total colonization of lands and people. Ironically, however, Durham's very refusal to be labelled as indigenous is read within the art market as confirmation of his indigenous status. Because the works of indigenous artists such as Jimmie Durham in the US, Gordon Bennett in Australia and Robert Jahnke in New Zealand unsettle the binary distinction between western art and indigenous art, there is always a danger that they will be viewed as either one or the other rather than as both; they must constantly resist the tendency of the art market to particularize them by displacing them towards the indigenous pole of the western/indigenous binary. Again caught in a binary not of their own making, they risk becoming, not so much an excluded, as a displaced middle. Durham's plea is: 'I'm still as authentic as I used to be but I'm trying to speak about you here. I'm trying to be here; would you please allow me to be here at this moment and forget wherever we both might have been yesterday.'[21]

Of course, we can never wholly be here now. But Durham is highlighting the historical nature of oppressive authenticity; it not only binds indigenous identities to traditional pasts, it also employs out-dated racial schemes that cannot possibly accommodate the diversity of contemporary indigenous life.

Biological authenticity is usually accompanied and reinforced by an oppressive cultural authenticity within post-settler states. To the north, in Canada, an earlier requirement of cultural authenticity for indigenous people has recently combined with blood politics to ensure that the number of culturally authentic Indians declines over time.

In 1876, eleven years before the Dawes Act, the Canadian Parliament passed the Indian Act, which, like the United States and Australian legislation, was intended to facilitate the assimilation and cultural elimination of indigenous people. It sought to do this by distinguishing between two categories of Indian – status Indians and non-status Indians – and by putting in place a mechanism whereby the number of status Indians would inevitably decrease over time. Status Indians were those who belonged to bands and lived on reserves. Non-status Indians were neither reserve Indians nor settlers: they belonged to an anomalous category that the 1876 Act officially excluded. This group would have no rights to government assistance and support that derived from treaty relationships with Indian bands. The Act provided for the expansion of this disenfranchised category through a clause stating that, when a woman married a non-status man, she and her children became non-status. When women married out of bands they were seen to be moving permanently into white society and there was to be no going back for them or their children.

Over the next hundred years many thousands of Indian women and children were denied full recognition of and access to their Indian heritage as the notion of two classes of Indian became set in official concrete. Today, approximately 200,000 Indians live on reserves while twice that number of non-status Indians live off reserves, mainly in southern urban centres.

In 1985, in an apparent move to address the injustices of the 1876 Act, the Canadian Parliament repealed the offending section so that it now became impossible to gain or lose status through marriage. This has since enabled more than 100,000 people who had lost status through the provisions of the 1876 Act to have their names added to the status register. However, in addition to repealing section 12(1)(b), Bill c-31 also ensures that the number of status Indians will continue to decrease in the longer term. Harry Daniels, former President of the Congress of Aboriginal Peoples, has suggested that Bill c-31 should be renamed the 'Abocide Bill' for this reason. Bill c-31 facilitates the elimination of status Indians by stipulating that, after two consecutive generations of marrying non-status Indians, the children of the third generation are not eligible for status. Officially, their blood will have become too diluted for them to be considered authentic Indians. This rule applies equally to women and men.

Why are the children of mixed marriages considered less socially authentic than those of non-mixed marriages? Because social authenticity for indigenous people is dependent on ancestry and ancestry is thought of as primarily a biological phenomenon. Here, an earlier requirement for social authenticity (living on reserves in ancestral communities) combines with new blood requirements to exclude future generations of indigenous children from official recognition. The new rules will also put pressure on status Indian communities to 'maintain the "racial" purity of their community and to discourage unions with non-status partners'.[22] The Bill is a generational time-bomb.

The requirement of cultural authenticity commonly excludes from official recognition indigenous people who do not belong to tribes. Ironically, the very concept of a 'tribe' is largely the creation of colonial administrations. British colonialism's most successful strategy, indirect rule, required officially recognized leaders of bounded groups occupying fixed areas of land. Chiefs, tribes and mapped territories were among the essential conditions of empire. Once officially defined, these groups took on a 'traditional' authenticity denied to other, 'non-tribal', groups that inhabited less clearly defined spaces. One of the contemporary legacies of the production of tribal authenticity is a denial of full official recognition to indigenous urban leaders and their organizations. Maori urban organizations in New Zealand and off-reserve Indian organizations in Canada and the United States, for example, have all consistently been denied the same level of government recognition and funding as that provided for rural-based tribal or band organizations. This is despite the fact that, as a result of the post-Second World War urban migrations, the majority of indigenous citizens in these countries now live in cities and towns: more than 80 per cent of Maori people live in urban areas; there are three times as many Canadian Indians (status and non-status) living off reserves as there are status Indians on reserves; and almost two-thirds of the 2 million Native Americans live off reservation in cities, towns and rural areas. Post-settler states have never fully included urban groups in deliberations over ways to achieve greater indigenous self-determination and the settlement of treaty grievances.

Oppressive cultural authenticity has recently been clearly evident in the exclusion of non-tribal Maori from shares in fishing assets in New Zealand. In 1992 Maori tribal representatives and the government reached an agreement that tribes would receive a half-share of a fishing company and a percentage of the fishing quota. In exchange, Maori would forfeit all rights to future fisheries claims against the government. A Fisheries Commission, comprising tribal representatives, was established to devise a fair model for allocation of the quota to tribes. It decided that quota would only be made available to authentic, officially recognized tribes, termed *iwi*, and that those Maori who did not affiliate with tribes (around 26 per cent of the Maori population) would receive nothing.

Urban Maori who would not or could not affiliate with *iwi* thus became an excluded middle, neither as fully individual as settlers nor as fully tribal as the Fisheries Commissioners and their constituencies. Urban Maori organizations unsuccessfully challenged the Commission's definition of authentic Maori society in the courts, arguing that they were as authentic as rural-based *iwi*; in fact, they claimed they *were iwi* in a contemporary form. John Tamihere, as head of one of the largest urban organizations, Te Whanau o Waipareira, publicly challenged official and popular views of tribally rooted authenticity by arguing that rural tribal leadership is backward-looking and that rural life represents a 'dead-end'. As a Catholic he said he did not feel the need to go to Rome, nor, as a member of the Ngati Porou tribe, did he feel the need to return to its ancestral lands on the east coast of the North Island. The future of Maori society is embodied, he claimed, in new urban groupings like his, which are able to take advantage of new opportunities offered by the global economy. For Tamihere, Maori success is dependent upon finding alternatives to traditional tribal structures, whereas for the Fisheries Commissioners it requires the perpetuation and strengthening of these structures. The Commissioners' views were supported by the courts and the government.

Post-settler governments support the perpetuation of tribes and tribal leaderships because it is only through dealing with these colonially recognized groups that illegitimate possession can be transformed into legitimate belonging for post-settler citizens. In negotiating land claims, therefore, governments would rather deal with a small number of tribal groups than with many smaller, residential groups. Post-settler states also prefer to devolve the delivery of welfare and other social services to these socially 'authentic' groupings. In New Zealand, for example, tribalism was given renewed official significance in the late 1980s and early '90s when, in order to create the appearance of greater indigenous self-determination, it was proposed to pass the delivery of social services over to officially authenticated tribes. The plans were soon abandoned, however, when it was realized that many of those who would require the services did know their tribe or were not active members of tribes. Tribes remain the main recipients of treaty-settlement money, however, and so now have a strong and enduring economic presence. There has been a significant growth in corporate tribalism as a result and tribal leaders, including those of Ngai Tahu in the South Island and Waikato in the North, now manage very large investments amounting to hundreds of millions of dollars derived mainly from treaty settlements.

As a result of a history of government-fostered tribalization in New Zealand, indigenous authenticity is now strongly tied to membership in *iwi*. Indeed, the hegemonic force of *iwi* ideology is now so strong that urban groups have been forced to claim that they, too, are types of *iwi*. Any third position between settler individualism and Maori tribalism appears unnatural and awkward, no matter how well founded it is in the realities of contemporary Maori life. The relationship between tribal and other Maori identities has become a troubling issue for those seeking greater recognition for an indigenous Maori nation. The Maori Congress, a tribally based national body established in 1990, has, since 1995, been struggling to reconcile a desire for greater tribal self-determination with the desire for a stronger collective Maori voice that transcends tribalism.[23] While it has concluded that 'the two need not be incompatible', the creation of formal structures that recognize both within a Maori nation has yet to be achieved. Many urban Maori organizations and those they represent, however, seek neither a collective Maori voice nor a tribal one. Instead, in seeking recognition as a legitimate new Maori voice they are questioning binary understandings of post-settler nationhood.

At the same time that authentic tribal belonging was being required in New Zealand in order to gain access to fish, authentic traditional belonging became a legal precondition for the recognition of Aboriginal land rights in Australia. In 1992 the Australian high court ruled that British possession of Australia in 1770 did not automatically extinguish native title; the assumption of *terra nullius*, literally 'empty land', upon which European settlement had been based, was declared invalid. In response to this judgement, popularly know as the Mabo decision, the Federal government passed the Native Title Act, which established a legal process through which Aboriginal people could claim lands wrongly taken from them by the Crown. However, a key provision of the Native Title Act was that claimants must be able to demonstrate a continuous traditional connection to the land being claimed. As might have been expected, the definition of 'traditional connection' has since become an extremely contentious issue in Australia; it is being debated in numerous forums, including, of course, the Native Claims Tribunal that was established to hear the claims of hundreds of Aboriginal communities.

The details of this debate need not concern us here. What is most significant is that this legislation defines many thousands of Aboriginal people as culturally inauthentic, as lacking a social quality that would allow them compensation for injustice. Indeed, many are now doubly disenfranchised; having been forcibly abducted from their communities, they are now prevented from re-establishing the severed connections with their land. Moreover, there is now a strong incentive for rural Aboriginal communities with claims to land based on traditional connection to accept this view tacitly and exclude urban people from their claim. There is, therefore, a clear parallel between conflicts that have arisen between urban and rural groups over land rights in Australia and disputes over fish quota in New Zealand.

In Canada, also, urban Aboriginal people are considered less culturally authentic than those on reserves, and have more restricted access to social services than reserve Indians. Despite the fact that almost half of all Aboriginal people in Canada live in cities and towns, a Royal Commission on Aboriginal People reported in 1999 that little thought had been given to improving their circumstances. Part of the explanation for this, the

Commission noted, was a deeply rooted perception that Aboriginal people belong on reserves or in rural areas. As a result of this government neglect, combined with recent strengthening of reserve-based institutions of governance and self-determination, many urban Aboriginal residents have become cynical. The Commission reported that many feel they have been pushed around by both whites and Indian elites and that they show their resistance by not participating in political events. Just as in New Zealand and Australia, new urban identities that are more than a bicultural blending of rural Indian and urban white are being created. But again, these are not adequately recognized in current models of indigenous social authenticity.

Of particular concern to the Commission was the fact that the urbanized half of Canada's indigenous population had been largely excluded from discussions about self-government and institutional development. It was clear that they had little collective visibility or power and that there was an urgent need to support the establishment of institutional structures that could represent and enhance their distinctive cultural identities. A very wide range of federally funded services is available for on-reserve Indians administered through local bands. These include education, health, policing, housing, economic development, alcohol rehabilitation, libraries, cultural centres, child and family services, recreation and senior citizens' programmes. Many of these are delivered in a culturally appropriate way with a high level of band control. Services for urban Indians fall well short of this. The Federal government has historically taken the view that its obligations ended at the reserve borders and that services to off-reserve Indians were the responsibilities of the provinces. Provincial jurisdiction therefore coincided with both a loss of Indian status and denial of culturally appropriate access to social services. Recent moves by the provinces to deliver targeted assistance to Indians have usually involved not the much needed establishment of new urban organizations but, instead, the devolving of service delivery to existing band organizations.

Urbanism and movement are today the predominant conditions of indigeneity. But indigenous urban life continues to be viewed officially as a dislocated, and hence anomalous, mode of existence. The corollary to this is that urban organizations and their leaders are not as fully included in wider cultural policy and constitutional debates as they should be. They are viewed with more suspicion and have more difficulty in gaining official recognition than 'traditional' rural-based groups. It seems that because the latter are more distinct from settler society they are viewed as more worthy beneficiaries of special economic support and political devolution.

In this chapter I have proposed that an oppressive authenticity has operated and continues to operate in the arenas of indigenous eco-politics, blood politics and tribal politics. Unless this politics of authenticity is somehow transcended, the future for geographically, genetically and culturally diverse indigenous peoples will be one of increasing exclusion through the operation of official and self-imposed binary distinctions: natural and unnatural; pure and impure; tribal and non-tribal. Part of the attraction of 'hybridity' for post-modernism lies in a desire to rattle the cages of binary thought. Perhaps, then, indigenous people should become more post-modern and embrace the notion of indigenous hybridity in order to escape their conceptual captivity? Perhaps, if we all accorded greater value to hybrid identities and celebrated those exciting, colourful mixtures that are being created in urban settings, the people in the middle would no longer face exclusion?

I do not think greater official or indigenous recognition of hybrid and indigenous identities is a solution to oppressive authenticity. The Aboriginal artist Julie Gough has noted that hybridity has become a western obsession at a time when the cultural purity of its centres is being threatened by migration from the peripheries; as she writes, 'the response to fear and uncertainty of change that the West is experiencing is the renaming and quantification of the other as "hybrid"'.[24] Hybridity is indeed a term reserved almost exclusively for others; it is a new conceptual tool for the maintenance of a binary distinction between indigenous otherness and the post-settler self.

Indigenous people are thus caught, once again, in a binary trap, not of their own making; they can choose to be other as hybrid or other as pure. It is, as Jimmie Durham found, very difficult for them to be themselves.

The politics of authenticity needs to be replaced by a politics of belonging and connection. Indigeneity is not primarily an individual biological or cultural identity; it is a mode of belonging to places, communities and nations. It is also a type of connection between people who belong to these places, communities and nations in indigenous ways. Indigenous belonging to places cannot be quantified – nor is it a question of either belonging or not belonging. Indigeneity, as a particular attachment to place, is a variable condition – it can be stronger or weaker at different times for different people in widely differing circumstances. Similarly, attachments to communities – rural and urban, on reserves and off reserves, on tribal land or away from tribal land – vary in strength throughout people's lives.

The great tragedy of the imposition of regimes of biological authenticity upon indigenous people is that it equated a sharing of blood with belonging within communities and nations. Yet 'half-caste' and 'quarter-caste' Aboriginal children belonged as securely within their families and to their communities as did 'full-blood' children. Non-status Indians in Canada did not sever their connections with relatives on reservations, nor did those Native Americans forced off reservations, because their blood quantum levels were too low, immediately break all ties with their more fortunate cousins. For some who were separated by blood politics, connections were lost or weakened over time, but connections can be re-established and strengthened. This is already happening in many parts of the indigenous world. Urban people in New Zealand, Canada and the United States are moving back to the country to discover their tribal roots; Aboriginal people are tracing their birth parents and discovering connections to the land.

Indigenous belonging in urban communities is not the same as indigenous belonging in rural communities, but it is nonetheless distinctive in relation to post-settler and migrant forms. Complex connections with rural kin and symbolic rather than active attachments to land and sea are maintained, often with difficulty given the demands of urban life. The great tragedy of the imposition of tribal authenticity is that a whole range of semi-tribal identities have been either excluded from official recognition or left undeveloped within post-settler states. De-tribalization was not cultural loss but cultural change; the continuities between urban and rural cultures have always been, and will continue to be, important for indigenous identity.

National belonging for indigenous people is a generalization and extension of more intimate forms of connection at another imaginary level. Eco-politics, blood politics and tribal politics operate as exclusionary discourses at this level because they invoke a binary relationship between the pure and the impure. Indigenous people are either too pure to belong to the mestizo nation or they are too impure to be indigenous. Rather than promoting indigenous modes of national belonging through strengthening a range of indigenous connections to place and community, the operation of oppressive authenticity has resulted in disconnection at all levels, including that of the national imagination.

The future of indigenous cultures will undoubtedly be one of increasing diversity. I have argued that unless post-settler states and indigenous leaders move beyond the contemporary politics of biological and cultural authenticity this cultural diversity will soon become the basis for new forms of oppression and exclusion. New forms of oppression and exclusion are already occurring in the arenas of eco-politics, blood-politics and tribal politics, and as urban indigeneity becomes the lived reality for increasing numbers of indigenous people they are likely to become more pervasive. Of critical importance for the future of indigenous cultures will be the development of a new politics of urban belonging and rural–urban connection. It is to be hoped that such a politics will draw more from kinship than bureaucratic reason – kinship has no excluded middles, only close relatives and more distant cousins.

# CHAPTER THREE

# Urban Indigeneity

Gathering outside my university building is a group of several hundred students, most of them Maori, who are preparing to march through the streets of Wellington to New Zealand's Parliament buildings. There, they will meet up with some 15,000 other protesters who have travelled from city suburbs and small rural communities throughout the country in order to voice their opposition to proposed legislation that will place the ownership of the country's foreshore and seabed firmly in government hands. The legislation will be a blatant confiscation, say the protesters' placards – many tribal rights to the sea have not yet been legally extinguished. Leading the protesters at Parliament will be a group of determined people who began their long march from a small rural community 600 kilometres away some two weeks ago. Their protest snowballed as they moved down the North Island, so that what began as a rural protest march is now climaxing as an historic urban and national occasion. Events such as this remind us that contemporary indigenous politics are the product of both rural and urban struggles and that the indigenous voice is loudest in the cities.

It is too often assumed that indigeneity is an essentially rural condition and that settlers built the towns and cities, places in which indigenous people don't really belong. This view is quite misleading. True, in the early part of the twentieth century settlers tended to be more urbanized than indigenous peoples, but for most of their histories the vast majority of both settlers and indigenous people has lived in rural communities. In 1800 only 2.2 per cent of Europeans lived in cities with populations of 100,000 or more. Rapid urbanization began with industrialization in the nineteenth century, first in Britain, where 40 per cent of the population was urban by 1900, and a little later in the rest of Europe. This massive relocation of people to cities within Europe and to overseas destinations (50 million people left Europe permanently between 1800 and 1914) was frequently accompanied by poverty. But it also required enormous cultural creativity as migrants reinvented their lives in their new environments.

The nationalisms of the nineteenth century were, in part, driven by the desire to contain and homogenize the cultural and social diversity that had been mobilized with urbanization and industrialization – languages were standardized, common education systems were introduced and hegemonic moral orders were promulgated. It was certainly not the case that migrants left their cultures in their rural villages in order to take on new national ones in the cities or that they became assimilated into a pre-existing urban culture. Migration always meant ongoing accommodations between diverse regional languages and cultures and engagements between these and the developing cultures of the nationalizing middle classes.

Indigenous urbanization, which followed post-settler urbanization in the second half of the twentieth century, was also associated with both impoverishment and at least as much cultural creativity as had character-ized the earlier urbanization. Yet many observers have seen only cultural loss. It has too readily been assumed that indigenous cultures are too fragile to survive in the cities; that they need to be nurtured in rural back-waters where people know who they are and where they belong. Indigenous cultures need to have their roots in the soil, it is said. Indigen-ous urbanization is seen as a fatal uprooting, the final stage in a long process of assimilation into the heart of the post-settler nationhood. But cities do not magically strip indigenous people of their cultural distinctiveness in order that they might join the working masses or the ranks of the unemployed. In their jobs or joblessness, in their housing and their social activities indigenous people are not destined to become merely urban workers, distinguishable from other urban workers only by their appearance.

What the nostalgic view overlooks is that indigenous people are as culturally creative and adaptable as anyone else. Eric Wolf made this point most forcefully in his book *Europe and the People without History*. His title was ironic: of course the people colonized by Europe have dynamic histories that include centuries of engagement with other peoples, including Europeans. These centuries of engagement are also centuries of cultural change – new organizations have been formed, new concepts have been invented, new identities have been negotiated, and new material environments have been assembled. Precisely the same can be said for indigenous migrants in the latter half of the twentieth century, and none of this activity represents cultural loss – quite the opposite in fact. The organizations, concepts, identities and material environments are always expansions and elaborations, in new contexts, of the wider indigenous culture. Thus, rather than view indigenous urbanization as a misguided act of cultural self-destruction or as a final surrender to the forces of assimilation, it is more helpful to view it, at least initially, as a *relocation* of indigeneity.

I mean relocation in its literal, geographic, sense and also as a metaphor for social change. Urbanization, as a physical relocation from one residence to another, commonly involves changes in domestic living arrangements within and between households mediated by differently constructed environments. It also commonly increases the physical distance between generations as grandchildren move away from their grandparents. We shouldn't underestimate the level of cultural creativity required of this geographic relocation.

But relocated indigeneity is much more than a matter of space. Most significantly, it is a relocation of indigenous people within national and global economies – a change in their class positions – requiring new forms of social organization and leadership. Relocated indigeneity may remain kin-ordered, but the nature of this order and its associated ideas and values may be significantly different from rural indigeneity. Material and expressive cultural forms are the more obvious manifestations of this reordering. Exciting new musical forms are created, such as Maori rap or chichi, the latter fusing local Andean music with international pop rhythms and singing of the experience of migration to cities such as Lima. New linguistic forms are created, such as those that combine Spanish with Mayan or Quechua grammatical structures or others that combine English with elements of Maori or Aboriginal syntax. But even more than this, rural tradition becomes a source for urban identities that are nurtured through a new politics of nationalized indigeneity.

In emphasizing the cultural creativity of relocated indigeneity I do not want to suggest that rural indigeneity is any less contemporary or that it is more fully an embodiment of timeless traditions. The rapid proletarianization that characterized nineteenth-century Europe was associated, throughout much of the indigenous world, with a process of peasantization that was politically driven through the imposition, by settler states, of systems of private land ownership. Peasantization resulted in massive land alienation as states confiscated 'surplus' land and as people sought relief from mounting private debt burdens, but it also required radical changes in social organization and symbolic life. In New Zealand, for example, following the individualization of Maori land ownership and the subsequent increase in the spatial separation of houses, Apirana Ngata encouraged the building of elaborately carved meeting-houses set on *marae* – sacred reserves where people meet for ritual occasions and to host groups of visitors. Meeting-houses on *marae* are now widely regarded as the epitome of ancient Maori tradition (indeed, they do have ancient precedents), but they are also expressions of the radical social change that took place in rural Maori communities during the latter half of the nineteenth century.

Similarly, the carved totem poles that represented the chiefly crests and ancestry of Kwakwaka'wakw (also known as Kwakiutl) leaders, whose people live on Canada's north-west coast, became larger and more elaborately carved in the late nineteenth century. The first of the heraldic tree-trunks in a Kwakwaka'wakw village dates from the early 1870s, carved during a period that saw a dramatic intensification of political rivalry. This was due to the increased ability of non-chiefly individuals to acquire western goods and challenge established chiefs in the large ceremonial exchanges known as potlatches. These were banned by the Canadian government in the mid-1880s; in 1921 the government confiscated masks and other valuables from Chief Dan Cranmer's potlatch and prosecuted the participants. The ceremonies were continued clandestinely, however, and since the removal of legal restrictions in 1951 they have been performed at least annually. In 1979 the government returned the objects seized from Chief Cranmer and these are now housed in two new tribal centres. The carved poles and ceremonial exchanges, like Maori meeting-houses, had traditional precedents but, again, individualization encouraged a dramatic reshaping of tradition that has since come to epitomize a rural cultural distinctiveness.

So when we compare rural with relocated indigeneity we are not contrasting the static with the dynamic. We are, instead, contrasting locations – both physical and social. Indigenous rural locations are almost always physically remote. Socially, they are also on the fringes of global and national economies, and this means that they often need to be propped up by government welfare payments. Relocated indigeneity can be viewed, positively, as an overcoming of this remoteness and the economic marginality that was forced upon rural communities in the nineteenth century and the early twentieth. Of course, it can also be viewed negatively. Relocated indigeneity is typically associated with increased racism and social stress.

But these conditions, like remoteness and marginality, have not simply been suffered by indigenous people. They have provided the impetus for new forms of identity politics and political action mobilized by new concepts and alternative styles of leadership.

In addition to physical and social relocation, urbanization also relocates indigeneity within the imagined national community. When indigeneity is a largely rural condition it is possible to imagine the nation as, in essence, a settler or post-settler community that has indigenous people on its fringes. It is also possible for indigenous communities to imagine themselves as squeezed out to the margins by settlers. Both spatial metaphors become less convincing with indigenous urbanization. Instead, new images suggest themselves: a post-settler nation whose centre is being occupied by indigenous peoples; rural indigenous communities as original hubs linked to new and expanding satellite communities. The former has been associated with notions such as the 'Indian problem' in Canada or *la mancha India* (the Indian stain) in Peru. The latter hub image is tied to much more positive visions of increasingly nationalized and internationalized indigenous connections and identities.

There has, however, been a wide variation in the extent to which this spatial re-imagination has incited a deeper rethinking of the relationship between nationhood and indigeneity. In the United States, Australia and Canada, where multicultural images dominate, indigenous urbanization is simply an enrichment of the mix and has not led to fundamental changes in the ways in which the nation is represented. In New Zealand, on the other hand, Maori urbanization has coincided with a rethinking of the nation as fundamentally bicultural rather than monocultural or multicultural. In Latin America multiculturalism has a different meaning in relation to oppressive ideals of culturally homogenous mestizo or ladino nationalisms. Here urban-based indigenous movements have pushed for redefinitions of their nations as multicultural and multi-ethnic democracies within which indigenous identities can have more secure locations.

Kin-based organizations in rural communities determine relationships between people and their land. Membership of such communities, defined in terms of marriage and descent, almost always gives access to land and rights to use other natural resources. Initially urban organizations retained their kin basis, but shifted the function of kinship away from land access to social services and support for fellow migrants. Throughout the indigenous world women have been at the forefront of these developments. In Peru, Chile and Guatemala, for example, women have been radicalized through military oppression – including systematic rape and murder of husbands and sons – and so in these countries mutual support was directly linked to political resistance. As one Mayan woman noted, 'before, as wives, when we went to the town we would not even think of ascending the steps of the town hall. Now we not only ascend the steps, we talk to the Mayor.'[1] And today, in the Mayan highlands of Guatemala, most mayors are themselves indigenous. In Lima there are more than 6,000 grass-roots organizations representing villages and districts that are headed by women and assisting with the provision of basic needs such as food, housing, sanitation, health care and education. As neo-liberal economic reforms began to bite in the late twentieth century, organizations such as Comedores Populares (soup kitchens) and Glass of Milk Committees, providing milk for children, came to serve essential social welfare functions.

In New Zealand, the Maori Women's Welfare League, which was formed in 1951 during the early years of urban migration, was the first truly national lobby group to address the social problems confronted by indigenous city dwellers. Its early focus was on Maori health and housing conditions and its members were extremely effective in pressuring governments to increase spending in these areas. While it is by no means a radical organization, some of its members were at the forefront of the more confrontational protests, especially those that took place during the 1970s and '80s. In 1975 its first president, Dame Whina Cooper, led a well-publicized 'land march', which travelled the length of the North Island demanding an end to the alienation of Maori land. The protesters I describe at the beginning of this chapter consciously modelled their protest on the march led by Whina Cooper, carrying the same flag borne by her marchers. The League continues to be a major player in New Zealand national politics with branches throughout the country. Perhaps its greatest strength is its ability to mediate rural and urban interests and transcend tribal differences.

These examples of women's leadership could be multiplied a thousand times for the rest of the indigenous world; in Australia, Canada and the United States indigenous women's organizations are leading struggles against violence within their own urban communities; they comprise the vast majority of teachers in indigenous schools; they are at the forefront of movements to improve indigenous health, designing and controlling alternative health systems. The gendered division of labour that characterizes rural indigeneity is less of a constraining force for women in urban contexts. Instead, they find new economic locations within the proletariat or middle class, working alongside men while being subjected to new forms of racism and sexism. This relocation process (combined with military oppression in some Latin American countries) has, in general, radicalized indigenous women more deeply than men. Rigoberta Menchu, winner of the Nobel Prize for Peace and author of *I, Rigoberta Menchu: An Indian Woman in Guatemala*, Haunani-kay Trask, Hawaiian activist and author of *From a Native Daughter*, and Donna Awatere, author of *Maori Sovereignty*, are just three of the many indigenous women who have drawn upon their grassroots participation in urban organizations to articulate the indigenous cause in national and international forums.

While women tend to be the driving forces behind many urban, grassroots organizations, men have tended to receive greater recognition from post-settler states as representatives of rural and urban communities. Men are, therefore, more likely to head national organizations to which governments have devolved power and decision-making. The National Indian Brotherhood in Canada and most US Indian tribal administrations are male-dominated, as are the New Zealand Maori Council and the Aboriginal and Torres Straight Islanders Commission. In some cases this situation means that, in addition to struggling against the state, women also need to win the support of indigenous men who hold positions of power. Selective state patronage was always divisive in rural communities and its legacy is no less so in urban contexts.

Urban, grass-roots organizations are, of course, not confined to addressing problems peculiar to women and families. However, many of the problems that these organizations seek to address – violence, drug use, alcoholism, youth suicide, imprisonment, family breakdown – have their roots in destructive and self-destructive male behaviours. Unable to achieve economic success or status within non-indigenous organizations, and unable to find a place within the rapidly changing indigenous society, urban men are more likely to direct their anger inwards, either onto themselves or their families. I know I am drawing this contrast between women and men too starkly, but the issue is, nonetheless, real and deeply troubling.

One of the more creative (if also destructive) responses by indigenous men to urban alienation is gang culture. In Canada, gangs such as the Indian Posse, Redd Alert, Warriors and Native Syndicate are expressions of extreme alienation and past educational abuse. These gangs provide an alternative status hierarchy to that of the dominant urban community and boundaries between them and the wider community – indigenous and non-indigenous – are strongly maintained through entry rituals and distinctive symbols of identity. The former may include 'beating in' and committing crimes to order; the latter may include the use of colours, hand signals and styles of clothing. Whereas in Canada and the United States indigenous gangs are small in comparison to larger gangs such as Hell's Angels, in New Zealand indigenous gangs have established dominance. Two gangs in particular, Black Power and The Mongrel Mob, have been building their organizations for 30 years and are now significant players – and rivals – in the local drug scene and the wider underground economy. Urban gangs, however, appeal to only a small minority of indigenous youth: a far greater number are involved in sports clubs, cultural groups and the indigenous music scene.

Dean Hapeta's story illustrates well the cultural struggles of indigenous youth to forge urban cultural forms that challenge both rural indigeneity and national identity. Raised in a predominantly working-class environment, Hapeta consciously rejected Maori gang culture in favour of cultural resistance rooted in reggae and hip-hop music. His group, Upper Hutt Posse, drew upon black American hip-hop to create an indigenous rap music that has influenced a generation of bands and fans across the country. By rapping in Maori about land issues and colonial history, his music has raised the political consciousness of audiences and helped redefine what it means to be Maori. While this music has since been embraced by non-indigenous youth, it remains a popular vehicle for promoting Maori language and values in urban settings. Under the name Te Kupu ('The Word'), Hapeta has released two versions of a solo album, *Ko Te Matakahi Kupu* ('The Words that Penetrate'), one in Maori and the other in English. Hapeta travels widely and for him, as for many others of his generation and background, indigeneity has a strong international dimension. 'I'm learning from all struggles', he says, 'getting out of my skin and coming back to share, as an ambassador for the Maori people.'[2]

Hapeta does not locate the origins of his political consciousness in the 'cultural awakening of the 1970s when the middleclass discovered its roots'; instead, he claims to have 'followed the learning curve of the streets'. While Hapeta and his generation have probably been more strongly influenced by their urban, working-class environments than their 'middleclass' forebears, I don't think however, that the influence of the activists of the 1970s can be so easily dismissed. It was their movement, like others initiated throughout the indigenous world in the early 1970s, that greatly increased public support for the 'preservation' of indigenous languages and cultures and the addressing of land rights issues. The indigenous movements of the

1970s were influenced in turn by the success of the civil rights movement in the United States and other new social movements that represented a shift to a new form of politics – a new political paradigm.

In most post-settler democracies prior to the mid-1960s an old paradigm of welfare-state consensus had prevailed within which the key political values were growth and security. Economic growth was assumed to be continuously possible and, accordingly, political debate centred on the distribution of rewards via the welfare state and union-management bargaining. Security was provided through government welfare, national defence and domestic law and order. This dual focus upon growth and security coincided with an emphasis upon civil privatism – politics was the domain of political institutions and trade unions and the majority of the population involved themselves in a de-politicized sphere of work, leisure and family-centred consumption. By the early 1970s, however, insecurity and the destructive consequences of growth had become issues for new social movements – the peace movement, women's movements and environmental movements in particular. As these largely middle-class movements developed critiques of the monolithic imposition of state power and the assumptions of western rationality and progress, they also opened up a political space within which indigenous issues could be more forcefully articulated. Many new social movements consciously placed a high priority on the inclusion of indigenous participants and their concerns but, in the final analysis, other agendas always took precedence over indigenous ones. For indigenous peoples, alliances with the new middle class were no less compromising than those with the old left.

Indigenous cultural movements were often an urban politics of relocation. Their concerns were the loss of language and culture, institutional racism, and the alienation of indigenous youth, all of which had been highlighted by urbanization. In the United States the American Indian Movement (AIM) was born out of the alienation experienced by the children of people relocated to such cities as Minneapolis in the 1950s. Founded in

1969, and drawing its support from the prisons and ghettos of Minneapolis, AIM introduced a new form of dramatic protest that made the front pages of newspapers and provided striking images for television stations. In November 1969 protesters representing Indian people in general, rather than particular tribes, occupied the island of Alcatraz, five years after the prison had been closed down, and claimed it by 'right of discovery'. In 1972 AIM members participated in a cavalcade of cars that converged on Washington to demand the return of Indian Sovereignty. The cavalcade went by the name of the 'trail of broken treaties', recalling the 1832 'trail of tears' when 16,000 Cherokee were forced to march from Georgia to Oklahoma, causing more than 3,000 deaths from cold and starvation. The following year, AIM members occupied the settlement of Wounded Knee, South Dakota, where more than 200 Sioux had been massacred by US cavalry in 1890. The 71-day siege attracted huge media attention for the indigenous cause.

Urban-based indigenous movements gained national prominence in many other post-settler states in the early 1970s in the wake of the AIM protests and the successes of the American civil rights movement. While the movements in each place addressed concerns specific to their political contexts, there was also a great deal of sharing of ideas and protest strategies. The formation of the World Council of Indigenous Peoples facilitated communication between organizations and an expanding network of informal contacts between urban-based leaders soon developed. Occupations of land and other significant sites were particularly effective in attracting media attention because they were public events and unsettled the certainties of colonial settlement. In Australia and New Zealand tent embassies were set up inside the grounds of their respective Parliaments; in Hawai'i, the island of Kaho'olawe was occupied by activists protesting against its use by the US Navy for bombing practice. Parallels were drawn between the desecration of Kaho'olawe and the bombing, again by the US Navy, of the Puerto Rican island of Vieques as alliances were formed between indigenous peoples from US possessions, territories and trusteeships.

Urban-based leaders drew upon connections with rural land and kin to politicize indigenous identities in new ways. While there had been many forms of rural resistance to colonial administration and force, these were invariably localized responses. The protests of urban-based organizations were presented and read as national responses challenging the foundations of post-settler nationhood in a more generalized and profound sense than before. Relocated indigeneity became a nationalized indigenism as these movements built organizations that transcended community and tribal boundaries.

Typically, the building of a national indigenous consciousness proceeded through distinct phases, beginning with an articulation of a generalized cultural distinctiveness and subsequently elaborating models of sovereignty and increased indigenous autonomy that drew their legitimacy from culturalist discourse. The Hawai'ian sovereignty movement, for example, began in the early 1970s with a focus on the cultural connections between indigenous people and their land and sea. The concept of *aloha 'aina* (love for the land) became the central organizing idea that underpinned a tradition-based distinctiveness. The organizers of the Kaho'olawe protests described the meaning of *aloha 'aina* as follows:

> Aloha 'aina is a traditional concept that lays the foundations for Hawaiian religion, culture and lifestyle. Aloha means love and 'aina means land. The two words together express several levels of meaning. At the deepest level, the presence of our ancestors and gods of the land are acknowledged, respected and cherished through ceremonies, both public and private. This intimacy with the 'aina is also expressed in the interdependent subsistence relationship between man and his island. Man is nurtured with taro from the land and fish from the sea, and in turn cultivates and

nourishes the island. This relationship is finally symbolized by
pride in our homeland – patriotism for this land Hawai'i.[3]

The notion of Hawai'ian sovereignty and the independence of Hawai'i
from the United States, first articulated in 1974, was informed by this
view that native Hawai'ians had a closer affinity to land and sea than other
inhabitants. Indigenous cultural links to the sea were most dramatically highlighted through the voyage of the traditional double-hulled canoe *Hokule'a*
from Hawai'i to Tahiti in 1976. An elaborate traditional ceremony marked the
launching of the canoe and other traditions associated with voyaging were
revived for the occasion. These drew upon a range of sources, including a
sketch of a ritual mask made by Captain Cook's artist, John Webber.

During its early years the ideals and philosophy behind Hawai'ian
sovereignty were articulated most clearly by urban intellectuals associated
with the University of Hawai'i. This does not mean that rural people were
not participants in the struggle – many battles to halt or reduce the destructive impact of tourist development were spearheaded by rural leaders.
However here, as elsewhere, the wider goals of the movement and the
identity politics that animated it were largely a product of intellectual
engagement and debate in and around the universities. Since the 1970s the
focus of the movement has shifted from cultural identity to the political
organization of sovereignty. Again, urban activists are playing a leading
role. The issue that has yet to be resolved is what form of political organization would best represent the culturally conceived nation. Proposed models
range from complete secession from the United States to autonomy in a
similar form to that of mainland Indian nations (the 'nation-within-a
nation' model) to an administrative body that would control and distribute
lease money from lands set aside for native Hawai'ians in the nineteenth
and twentieth centuries.

The elaboration of an urban indigenous consciousness – a nationalized
indigenism – has followed a remarkably similar course within all post-

settler states. This is due, in part, to the sharing of ideas between indigenous peoples, but it is also a reflection of a wider international acceptance of the need for states to recognize cultural difference. In other words, indigenous cultural nationalism has been encouraged by both state policy-makers and indigenous intellectuals – and they are sometimes the same people. In Bolivia, for example, the indigenous Vice-President, Victor Hugo Cardenas, rode a wave of cultural nationalism into the heart of the political system, articulating a new sense of Bolivian nationhood in the process. At his inauguration in 1993 he encouraged people to view Bolivia as a 'nation of nations', a 'pluricultural' country within which indigenous cultures could flourish. Cardenas's vision was that of an urbanized intellectual who, like many of his fellow activists, had moved from a rural community to La Paz in order to further his secondary and university education in the 1960s. As a member of the Kataristas, an urban organization dedicated to Indian autonomy, Cardenas elaborated and sought to give practical effect to a philosophy that came to be known as *Indianismo* (Indianism).

In the 1970s and '80s *Indianismo* became a basis for ideological unity for diverse urban and rural groups engaged in a range of cultural and social projects. Moreover, in Bolivia, Colombia and Ecuador, *Indianismo* has provided both a coherent nationalist framework and a basis for international alliances among indigenous peoples. Phillip Wearne has usefully distinguished three different schools of thought that have been dominant at different times since the 1970s.[4] First, and most prevalent in the 1970s and '80s, there was a view that indigenous values and beliefs were closely compatible with left-wing values and objectives. Because indigenous peoples comprised the majority of the oppressed and working class, workers' struggles through trade unions and armed guerrilla groups were also indigenous struggles. A second school of thought grew out of disillusionment with the politics of left and right, its followers choosing instead to elaborate a philosophy of cultural purity and a return to traditional organization. One of the ideals advocated was *Tawantinsuyu*, the cosmological order that underpinned the Inca state. A third school of thought within *Indianismo*, and one that is currently dominant, asserts that indigenous peoples should form their own organizations but that alliances are essential with other non-indigenous organizations in order to achieve particular goals. It was this centrist philosophy that Cardenas sought to promote in Bolivia.

The distinction between an indigenous cultural nationalism that recognizes the need for strategic class alliances and one that sees indigenous cultural autonomy as an issue quite separate from class-based inequality has parallels throughout the indigenous world. The rise of the Maori sovereignty movement in New Zealand, for example, followed a similar path to that of South American movements in that the politics of *Maoritanga* (Maori culture and identity) was uncoupled from class and union politics in the 1970s. Maori protest organizations in the early 1970s viewed racism as an outcome of class oppression and promoted the view that it was rich settlers rather than all settlers who were responsible for Maori oppression. The fundamental divide was between bosses and workers, not between Maori and Pakeha (descendants of settlers). This perspective was replaced by a radical culturalism at about the same time that *Indianismo* was becoming dominant in South American countries.

Leading the push for a greater recognition of *Maoritanga* by the New Zealand state and media, which was largely state-controlled, was a group of urban students and workers who took the name Nga Tamatoa ('the young warriors'). The movement was strongly influenced by American Black Power rhetoric that viewed the fundamental social divide as a racial or cultural one rather than one of class. This analysis appealed to the more middle-class intellectuals who came to dominate the leadership in the mid- to late 1970s. As in Hawaii, and indeed most post-settler states, the culturalism of the 1970s became, by the 1980s, a cultural nationalism within which there was virtually no recognition of the significance of class.

Indigeneity had been relocated to urban settings and in the process racism and settler monoculturalism had been thrown into stark relief.

These visible and immediate forms of oppression were not shared by other non-indigenous members of the working class – indeed they were often perpetuated by them – and so it is not surprising that the politics of left and right was rejected by indigenous leaders. What was needed was a 'new left' able to articulate the complex intersection between class and culture. What indigenous leaders got instead was the collapse of the left and the simultaneous rise of new social movements for which identity and the destructiveness of western rationality were the central issues. A critique of capitalism as the driving force of colonialism, and hence indigenous oppression, was replaced by a critique of western culture and its values of individualism, materialism and competitiveness. Identity politics would soon become the only game in town.

In their opposition to western rationality, indigenous peoples everywhere emphasized identities that were based on spirituality, tradition and sharing. Autonomy and sovereignty came to mean the freedom to express these identities and the ability to nourish them through re-establishing and strengthening symbolic and practical connections between people, land and sea, and connections between ancient pasts and the present. Enormous efforts are now being made by urbanized indigenous peoples to revive languages, to learn more about traditional medicine and calendars, religious rituals and traditional dances, and to pass this knowledge on to their children. In Latin America, for example,

> thousands of young men and women have started to demand training as shamans; printing presses have sprung up to satisfy a growing hunger for manuals, texts and folklore, often in indigenous languages. Those who cannot read are read to by their children or provide the material for others to 'formalize' the semi-secret spiritual world that has been at the heart of the almost invisible indigenous resistance for centuries.[5]

There is a strong and growing interest in indigenous schools among urban Maori. These kura kaupapa are widely regarded as among the most successful outcomes of the cultural movement begun by Nga Tamatoa and others in the 1970s. Initially the focus was on increasing the availability of Maori-language teaching in state schools and enhancing the status of Maori culture generally. But by the early 1980s this culturalism had fuelled a more ambitious cultural nationalism that sought to put in place an alternative indigenous education system embodying traditional Maori values and teaching practices. Kura kaupapa became a middle stage in an education system that began with kohanga reo ('language nests' for pre-schoolers) and ended with whare wananga (Maori universities).

A similar system was created in Hawai'i where punanga leo, modelled on the Maori kohanga reo, are the entry points. In addition, indigenous Hawai'ians have established numerous hula halau (traditional Hawai'ian dance schools) that have encouraged a flourishing interest in hula, tradi-tional and modern music, chant and oral traditions among urbanized people. Teachers and participants emphasize the spirituality of the hula and strongly disassociate their performance from the commercialized hula that is sold to tourists. For those who attend hula halau, hula is much more than dance. It nourishes an identity rooted in links to ancestor gods and the land. Religious) restrictions are observed and relationships between teachers and students follow traditional precedents.

Here again, urban culturalism feeds into cultural nationalism. Indigenous schools and hula halau raise the awareness of the extent to which the freedom to be an indigenous Hawai'ian is restricted by foreign structures and values. The Hawai'ian sovereignty movement builds upon this in charting a future distinct from that envisaged by state authorities. Ka Lahui, a leading sovereignty organization, defines sovereignty as 'the ability of people who share a common culture, religion, language, value system and land base to exercise control over their lands and lives indepen-dent of other nations'. A key condition is 'a strong and abiding faith in the akua [ancestor gods] because a spiritually empty people do not make a strong nation.' Hula halau and the spirituality that they nurture are therefore central to the Hawai'ian cultural nationalist vision.[6]

In Canada, friendship centres and cultural survival schools have become important urban sites for cultural learning and rediscovery by indigenous people. For many urban people the friendship centre is at the heart of their community, offering cultural programmes, access to information, services and contacts and providing an environment where indigenous people can feel good about themselves and their identity. Despite cultural differences, people point to a common spirituality that unites them in relation to the wider materialistic society. Cultural survival schools are flourishing in major cities such as Toronto and Edmonton where, like indigenous schools in New Zealand and Hawai'i, they constitute an alternative system to that of the public schools. Traditional knowledge and history is taught and valued, and students have opportunities to attend cultural camps run by elders in rural settings.

Friendship centres and indigenous schools have participated in a dramatic movement of cultural renewal and rediscovery across Canada over recent years. Sun dances, sweat lodge ceremonies, fasting, potlatches, traditional healing rituals and other ceremonies are being given new significance as expressions of indigenous identity in urban settings. For some, this has also meant re-establishing or strengthening links with rural kin, but not all urban dwellers have this option. The city has become a permanent home for many and rural life has become an idealized existence that they rarely experience. Whether 'home' is the city or the reserve, however, people are finding a basis for unity in the spiritual bonds that are strengthened through cultural revival and this is assisting with the building of political consensus and cooperation at the national level.

These examples of indigenous culturalism and cultural nationalism represent responses from urban people who have, often with good reason, been very reluctant to forge close alliances with both the 'old' working-class left and the 'new' middle-class left. An analysis that locates oppression in cultural difference and proposes liberation through cultural autonomy is unlikely to be greatly sympathetic to a politics of class or individual liberty. Moreover, practice has shown, time and again, that when indigenous voices are in the minority, whether within left-wing organizations or in the wider social field, they need to be loud ones – and people quickly tire of shouting. If indigenous organizations, however, eschew formal alliances with the political left, the cultivation of more generalized goodwill, if not positive support, within the wider population becomes absolutely essential.

Post-settler states and their wider populations have, in recent years, been more willing to support greater recognition of indigenous cultures – after all, it is relatively inexpensive and enhances the appearance of a national inclusiveness within which illegitimate dispossession has become legitimate belonging for both indigenous people and post-settlers. In response to indigenous cultural nationalism, governments have sought to make their public services more appropriate and 'user-friendly' to indigenous people. They have expanded the number of cultural advisers and promoted symbolic displays and public expressions of a cultural inclusiveness. All government departments in New Zealand, for example, have adopted Maori names – the Department of Inland Revenue became Te Tari Taake (The Tax Department) – and these names are now displayed on buildings, documents, official correspondence and in job advertisements alongside their English equivalents. Official pamphlets, booklets and policy statements are published in Maori and English, as are job advertisements in local papers. Maori ceremonial traditions have been adopted to mark official occasions and carved murals have been installed in some government offices.

Developments such as these have increased employment opportunities for some members of the indigenous middle class and have created the appearance of dramatic changes in the status of indigenous people within post-settler nations. For the most part, however, such changes have been illusory in that few indigenous people – urban and rural – have received tangible economic benefits from cultural window-dressing. Indigenous cultural nationalism has to be rooted in the lives of indigenous people as they are actually lived, rather than relying on cultural symbolism promoted by post-settler states in the interests of national harmony.

Officially promoted cultures tied to systemic priorities tend to become excessively formalized and standardized. When, in the name of purity, government agencies officially set and monitor adherence to linguistic and cultural guidelines there is a danger that new forms of oppressive authenticity will be created. In New Zealand, for example, a Maori Language Commission, established to foster Maori language use, published a bureaucrats' guide, *Maori for the Office*. It comprised three sections: office vocabulary (connected with people, layout, equipment and actions), writing business letters, and job advertising. This booklet was an attempt to standardize language use within an administrative context. Included in it were many newly coined words: *kopae pingore* (floppy disk), *kopae maro* (hard disk), *kaupapa topu* (corporate plan). There was also advice on how to express file references, Maori place names for correspondence, farewells to the dead (for beginning formal letters), Maori names for government departments and administrative positions, and exemplary letters and job advertisements. In producing this booklet the Commission was also standardizing the use of Maori language in corporate display and their endeavours were to have parallels in the codification of indigenous ceremonial practices within government.

Of course, in one sense, such standardization of indigenous culture by the state for symbolic purposes is a small price to pay for greater recognition of this culture nationally. However, it is by no means an entirely innocent or positive development. It reinforces a general misrecognition of lived urban indigeneity while at the same time containing the more radical demands of indigenous sovereignty organizations. Urban people who do not speak an indigenous language and who do not adhere to officially recognized traditions are viewed as less than authentic and their lived cultures are regarded as less worthy of official support.

In such contexts urban indigeneity has, therefore, two faces – a nationalized symbolic face whose features may be appropriated by post-settler states for objectives that may be in conflict with those of indigenous leaders, and a largely hidden face, often unrecognized as indigenous, in the poorer neighbourhoods and suburbs of the city. Only one of these faces is real; the other is a mask behind which the real face is hidden. Masked faces become necessary when post-settler states insist on dealing with standardized identities: they are the working fictions of oppressive authenticity, enabling colonizer and colonized to continue their dialogue and unequal exchanges. But these masks are useful for traditional indigenous leaders, too, in that they conceal social changes that threaten their authority. Tribal leaders have a significant stake in preserving the appearances of tribalism, especially when dealing with post-settler governments that are committed to settling long-standing tribal grievances.

The crucial issue for indigenous advocates of urban cultural change and more representative leadership structures will be finding ways to maintain strong alliances with rural communities while at the same time developing new ways of being indigenous. At present such alliances are hindered by government policies that seek to address colonial injustices through compensating tribes and rural communities. There has been a reluctance to accept that urban poverty and the associated social problems that many indigenous people face in cities have their roots in rural injustices – that rural and urban poverty comprise a single condition with common origins in land alienation and loss of self-determination. In general, post-settler governments need to involve more fully a wide range of urban and rural leaders in their negotiations over land claims and self-determination. There is more than a hint of divide and rule in the current approaches of many governments.

Indigenous politics is still too often viewed in terms of a binary relationship: tribe and settler. While this is the case, indigenous urban culture will continue to occupy a largely unrecognized territory between traditional and modern. Behind the masks of orthodoxy new urban cultural forms will continue to be produced, but unless they are tied to new forms of self-determination able to express urban and rural interests they will struggle to find acceptance within tribal and national regimes of cultural control. Urban and rural do not constitute two separate indigenous worlds – although it can often appear this way to the many people who have to make long and expensive journeys to visit relatives at 'home'. Relocated indigeneity may become dislocated indigeneity, but there is only one world, in which rural and urban indigenous people are joined at the hips.

# CHAPTER FOUR

# Indigenous Children

I don't know who first coined the term 'assimilation', but it is hard to conceive of a more inappropriate word to describe the disintegration of indigenous cultures and communities within settler states. In official and popular discourse the word evokes an entirely false image of a slow, quasi-natural, process through which individuals move from their birth group into a second, larger group, taking on, as they do so, the cultural characteristics of the larger group. Synonyms include 'amalgamation', suggesting a gentle coming-together of diverse peoples into a greater unity and harmony, and 'absorption' – sucking up or mopping up some liquid with a sponge. No hint of violence in any of these terms. But nothing could be further from the truth. Behind the apparently benign façades of assimilation, amalgamation and absorption is a terrible history of brutalization and genocide, a history that has been focused most intensively and devastatingly upon indigenous children.

Assimilation, conceived of as a joining or coming together, reflected the perspective of those who pursued settler nationhood. Viewed from the perspective of indigenous peoples assimilation was, instead, a *separation* –

often violent – of kin from kin, people from their homes, people from their cultures and, especially, children from their parents and families. Children became the particular targets of assimilative separation with the introduction, in the nineteenth century and the early twentieth, of forced education programmes. These were designed to supplement other forms of assimilative separation such as land alienation and resettlement programmes, and were usually introduced at about the same time as the latter measures. In the United States, for example, a one-two punch was delivered with the passing, in 1887, of both the Dawes Act and the Compulsory Education Act. As we have seen, the former was designed to alienate millions of acres of Indian land designated 'surplus' after individual allotments had been determined. The latter was intended to eradicate Indian languages and sever the affiliations of children to their families and tribes. As the Commissioner of Indian Affairs put it, the aim was 'to fuse' Indian peoples 'into one homogenous mass' through the only way possible – by separating them from their languages. 'Uniformity of language will do this', he said, 'nothing else will'.[1]

In New Zealand, also, a system of state-controlled Native Schools was introduced just two years after the establishment of the Native Land Court, the primary instrument for separating Maori communities from their land. Like the American schools, these were designed to transform tribally distinct peoples into a homogenous class of English-speaking labourers and tradesmen. The 1909 Aboriginal Protection Act gave the Australian government the power to force Aboriginal people onto reserves under strict controls and surveillance. The Act also officially sanctioned the separation of children from their reserve-confined families and their removal to missionary-run boarding schools. These schools, like those in the United States and Canada, were notorious for their rigid discipline and determination to extinguish the children's attachments to their original languages and cultures. The Aboriginal Protection Board, which carried out the surveillance and destruction of Aboriginal society under the Act, became known among some indigenous Australians as the 'Aboriginal Persecution

Board'. In Canada, state support for residential schools in the 1880s followed closely upon the passing of the 1876 Indian Act, which inaugurated a broad programme aimed at the ultimate 'extinction of Indians as Indians'. Schools were to assist in this process by stripping Indian children of their culture and 'civilizing' them in preparation for 'enfranchisement', the loss of official Indian status under the Indian Act.

Assimilative violence towards indigenous children was always, therefore, an intrinsic dimension of broader programmes aimed at community destruction and land alienation. It has had profound and lasting effects on generations of indigenous people, psychologically and socially. In the last thirty years, in hundreds of communities throughout the indigenous world, children have become the focus of language and cultural revival programmes aimed at fostering greater self-esteem and strengthening community identities. But in light of the massive scale of personal and social destruction visited upon these communities and their children in the past, such efforts cannot help but assume heroic proportions. Assimilation was not, as I have already insisted, a joining or merging of peoples into a larger whole, and so a reversal of the effects of assimilation is not going to be achieved by simply dividing communities and children from that larger whole. Because violent separation was so central to assimilation, the strengthening of inter-generational connections within and between rural and urban indigenous communities has to be a primary focus of indigenous social movements.

In this chapter I discuss the separation, through forced schooling, of indigenous children from their families and communities, and consider some contemporary examples of indigenous schooling that seek to address the legacy of assimilation. I suggest that we should not expect too much of indigenous schools and the dedicated staff who run them – schools don't make communities and nor do they necessarily strengthen them. Indigenous schooling must always be integral to a much broader social movement if it is to succeed in strengthening connections between children and their families and communities. All teachers within indigenous schools know this. Most governments do not wish to.

## Assimilation was Settlement

The transformation of children into citizens is one of the great on-going projects of nations everywhere. But why, in so many settler nations, has this required the cultural and physical separation of indigenous children from their communities? Why were indigenous children not simply left to become indigenous citizens in their own ways in their own homes? Part of the answer obviously lies in settler beliefs about their own cultural and linguistic superiority and the low status accorded to the languages and cultures carried by the parents of indigenous children. But this, in itself, cannot explain the obsessive drive for generational separation and cultural extinction; after all, working-class culture had long been denigrated by middle-class nation-builders. I think we come closer to understanding the origins of policies of generational separation when we recognize that they were not merely mechanisms for cultural extinction but that they were, more profoundly, aimed at the disintegration of whole indigenous communities.

Assimilation policies in settler nations were not merely efforts to produce culturally homogenous citizens; they were interventions into the social reproduction of indigenous communities in tandem with other policies that sought to remove these communities from their land or radically transform the relationship between indigenous people and their environment. The physical removal of children reflected, in a particularly condensed form, the wider processes of social separation taking place at the time.

In essence, therefore, *assimilation was settlement*. Where settlement required the physical separation of indigenous communities from their land through force and/or legislation, settler states were faced with the question of what was to become of the people displaced. Various temporary solutions were imposed. In Australia, Aboriginal people were forcibly confined to reservations where they were expected to die out quietly. In Canada and the United States, official recognition required continued residence on reservations from which, it was expected, Indians would leave to become generalized citizens. In other cases, such as New Zealand, no provision was made for displaced people – they were simply expected to die out, merge with the nation's rural labour force or become Europeanized farmers. Assimilation policies that employed educational separation generally followed an official recognition that the above measures would not, in themselves, address the problem of what to do with the dispossessed. Dispossession of land needed to be supplemented by the dispossession of culture.

Dispossession of culture was usually conceptualized, in official discourse, as natives taking possession of a new culture in order to become full members of the settler nation. Hence in New Zealand, in the 1930s, the attendance of Maori children in state schools was regarded as a sign that tribal control over land would soon give way to individualized land use and sales to Europeans. Maori would become settlers. A government commission of inquiry, whose findings forced the resignation of Apirana Ngata and reaffirmed the centrality of a policy of assimilation, put it this way:

> It is clear, of course, that the Maori settler cannot, in general, be regarded as a European. He needs and should evoke more sympathy, patience, understanding and friendly firmness. Yet for many years now the Maori people have been surrounded by influences which tend to what is called 'Europeanization' and the future must be affected by the present state of education among the young . . . over 90 per cent of the Maori children of school age are being educated in state primary schools [native and public], and that must be an important factor in the development of Native farming in the future.

The commission was firmly of the view that the expansion of settlement in New Zealand depended on the transformation of Maori into settlers, and that this required the simultaneous breaking down of tribal land ownership and tribal consciousness. State education of Maori children would achieve the latter.[2]

Popular and official discussions of assimilation are often infected with a pervasive culturalism and idealism that, if you will excuse the pun, I would like to unsettle here. By conceptualizing assimilation as settlement we emphasize the social and material motivations of state policies rather than the presumed effects in the heads of indigenous people. Dispossession of land was mirrored in the dispossession of children and both were fundamental to state projects of settlement. By thinking assimilation and settlement together we also highlight the fact that assimilation had a bodily dimension in that it included forced movements of people, including children, from one place to another; that it physically separated people from each other and their environment in order that others might take their place; that assimilation was geographic displacement as much as it was cultural loss. By physically removing indigenous children from their communities, settler governments and churches were asserting a form of temporary ownership over them at the same time as they were asserting their permanent ownership over indigenous land. More than this, they were claiming ownership over indigenous children *in order* to claim ownership over indigenous land. The alienation of land required the alienation of children.

For both indigenous communities and settler governments, children represented the future. But of course each imagined their futures very differently. In enforcing the separation between children and their parents, settler governments and churches sometimes deluded themselves that this was not dispossession, but instead a sort of temporary adoption through which indigenous children would gain a better future than might have been granted to their parents. In most cases, of course, the children's futures were no better than those of their parents; frequently they were worse. And more often than not, the future of indigenous people was subordinated to the much grander future of the settler nation, a community to which indigenous children did not yet fully belong. So in a very real sense, by now reclaiming their children, indigenous communities are today claiming back their right to create alternative indigenous futures to those originally envisaged by settler nations. It is no accident that this repossession of children is pursued at the same time as the recovery of land. Indeed, for many indigenous communities the repossession of children requires the repossession of land as a place where they can be nurtured.

Before considering some indigenous attempts to reclaim their children and their futures through indigenous schools, let me first briefly review the educational legacy of dispossession and separation that they seek to overcome. It is only by gaining an understanding of the scale of the separational violence that was directed towards indigenous children and their communities that we can fully appreciate the enormity of the tasks facing these schools.

Settler-state schooling systems of the nineteenth and twentieth centuries varied considerably in their levels of brutality towards indigenous children and in the degrees of separation produced and maintained between the children and their families. All routinely employed physical and psychological violence, however, and encouraged the severing of intergenerational ties. In Australia, the United States and Canada the physical separation of indigenous children from their parents and their confinement in distant boarding schools greatly magnified their cultural separation from their communities.

In Australia, as in New Zealand and the United States, the alienation of children from their communities was preceded by the alienation of people from their land. The establishment of large pastoral stations by European settlers in Australia was accompanied by almost unimaginable brutality towards indigenous people. Deborah Bird Rose put it succinctly: 'There were few choices. In the early years, people worked for Europeans, or resisted. Those who resisted, or were simply in the way, were shot, beaten to death, poisoned.[3] Entire Aboriginal communities were forced to leave their ancestral lands and relocate near mission stations under strict controls and surveillance. Here children became the special targets of missionary endeavours. Many were held captive in mission schools, where they suffered physical abuse or died from contagious diseases that spread rapidly in the crowded and profoundly alien conditions. The massive population decline from the 1840s onwards was viewed by church leaders, however, as confirmation that Aboriginal people were unfit to survive in the modern world.

Little wonder there was widespread resistance to mission education among these profoundly dislocated communities. One missionary complained:

> I lament much that the difficulty to obtain Aboriginal children for instruction has increased almost to an impossibility . . . The parents conceal their children as soon as they hear that a missionary approaches their camp; and when I have come upon them by surprise I have the grievance to observe these little ones running into the bushes or into the bed of the river with utmost speed.[4]

Such resistance kept most Aboriginal children out of the hands of church educators for much of the nineteenth century; the forced confinement, however, of Aboriginal people in government reserves in the early twentieth century initiated a new era of child abduction. By the middle of the century most of the Aboriginal population had been forced onto some 70 reserves on the fringes of white society. Living conditions were deplorable and families quickly became trapped in a life of poverty and hopelessness that would afflict generations. But life was no better for the tens of thousands of children who were forcibly removed from these reserves and confined in distant missions. By the 1950s, in Western

Australia, these missions 'stretched in a great arc the length of the vast state, providing every significant country town with such a facility'.[5] Missions were run on a dormitory style and with minimum staff. Discipline was rigid and frequently cruel. For many children life was one of physical torment and emotional trauma as the mission staff worked to break their cultural attachments to their families and communities. It is wholly unsurprising that many turned to alcohol and crime when they were released from captivity at 16 years of age. And, of course, they also began having children of their own.[6]

A leading advocate of assimilation through generational separation in the United States was Captain Richard Henry Pratt, one of a group of idealistic, if misguided reformers associated with the boarding schools movement in the 1880s. Carlisle Indian School, which he founded in 1879, became a model for hundreds of similar schools that were established throughout the country between 1880 and 1920. By the 1930s almost one-third of all Indian children were being educated in boarding schools either on or off the reservations. Pratt's dictum was 'kill the Indian and save the man', and his schools were designed to effect the total transformation of Indian children into Europeanized, English-speaking adults. 'Before and after' photographs were taken of the pupils to illustrate the supposed success of the ventures; long hair became short, traditional dress became Victorian, bodily posture became more upright.

One of the justifications for assimilation through education was that it was less expensive than military force. Around the turn of the century the Federal government sought to reduce costs further by establishing boarding schools and day schools on reservations while continuing to fund schools off reservation. In the reservation boarding schools contact between parents and children remained severely restricted: students stayed for nine months of the year and parents made brief visits at scheduled times. All boarding schools, on and off reservation, were run along military lines – children were marched to and from classes and were divided into companies. Punishment, which included beatings and humiliation, was usually harsh. Speaking in native languages was prohibited and incurred severe punishments. The schools operated what came to be known as a 'half-and-half' system in which formal lessons were held in the morning and vocational and domestic training was provided in the afternoons. Boys learned farming, gardening and woodwork and contributed to the running of the schools through manual labour. Girls learned sewing, cooking and cleaning and also assisted with school maintenance.

As in Australia, there was widespread resistance to educational separation and dispossession in the early years. This took the form of parental concealment of children on the one hand and escapes by children from schools on the other. Strong pressure was brought to bear on parents to give up their children, however, especially after 1893 when education became compulsory. Government payments and rations could be withheld from families who did not comply with the law and school police hunted down escaping children. A Navajo elder recalled one such hunting down:

> THOMAS JAMES: I had just gotten to school [at Chinle]. I hadn't been there a month, maybe about two weeks, when some boys asked me to run away during the night . . . We went straight to the road down the hill, a place called Ma'iitohi [Coyote Wash], in between the rocks. Just as we started toward it, a horse appeared behind us on the hill. It was a man named Kenneth. He had whip with him . . . [after attempting to elude him] two of us started off and ran as fast as we could straight back to school.
>
> INTERVIEWER [Laughing]: Having gotten scared of him?
>
> THOMAS JAMES: Yes, we got scared . . . I guess while he was chasing the [other] boys on his horse, he ran over one of them. The boy died.[7]

As was the case for Maori in New Zealand, most American Indian children were being educated in the public schools by the 1920s. Indigenous children usually constituted minorities within these schools, which, like all public schools within settler states, made no provision for indigenous cultures or languages. As increasing numbers of parents began to send their children to urban public schools, government boarding schools began to close down – most had done so by 1940. Greater control over the remaining schools was devolved to tribes, which, by the 1970s, had radically transformed their management and teaching practices. Only a handful of off-reservation schools remain today and most of the reservation boarding schools are on one reservation – that of the Navajo people. Navajo have been at the forefront of innovative approaches to education and later in this chapter we will look briefly at the attempts by one Navajo community to achieve greater self-determination in schooling.

Across the border, in Canada, Pratt's schools became models for state-funded residential schools in the early 1880s. Like those in the United States, these were explicitly designed to eliminate Indian identities and hence cut back on specific financial obligations that the state had towards Indian peoples. Schools would be, in the long run, cheaper than other forms of violence. Between 1883 and the 1920s some 80 residential institutions across Canada became integrated into a pedagogical archipelago under the surveillance and sponsorship of the Department of Indian Affairs. Although residential schools were initially supported by some Indian bands, their support quickly evaporated as the institutions developed reputations for harsh treatment, physical abuse and death: between 1894 and 1908 almost a third of the indigenous children in these schools died, mainly of infectious diseases.[8]

While the Canadian schools were similar to those in the United States in their enforcement of a separation between children and their parents – and, hence, between children and their cultures – and in their daily routines and levels of violence, the continued involvement of the churches was a distinctive feature of the Canadian system. As in all settler nations, the involvement of the churches in indigenous assimilation through education predated the setting up of a government-funded system. But whereas church involvement in New Zealand and the United States was largely discontinued by the twentieth century, in Canada and Australia all residential schools continued to be run by the churches on behalf of the government. In Canada early church educators, including the Protestant Church Missionary Society and the Catholic Jesuits, used indigenous languages in their religious services and schools, but by the end of the nineteenth century government pressure had forced such practices to be officially abandoned in residential institutions.

A Royal Commission on Aboriginal Peoples, established in Canada in 1996, investigated and documented the physical and sexual abuse suffered by indigenous children in residential schools and concluded that it was widespread and systematic. Following the presentation of the Commission's report, the Canadian Minister of Indian Affairs acknowledged the great harm that had been done and apologized on behalf of the Government. Church leaders have also been forced to apologize following publication of evidence that they and their predecessors knew of the abuse but did nothing to stop it. Apologies needed to be matched by substantial compensation payments: thousands of lawsuits claiming hundreds of millions of dollars have since been filed. Churches were threatened with bankruptcy, but the Canadian government has since agreed to pay most of the compensation for proven cases of abuse. Among those charged with crimes have been former members of the Royal Canadian Mounted Police, whose job it was to round up Indian children and forcibly abduct them from their homes and communities.

One of the less oppressive settler-controlled regimes was the Native Schools system established in New Zealand in 1867. Primary schools for children in rural Maori communities were established in the immediate aftermath of military invasions and occupations by government troops of

Maori tribal territories in the central North Island. Together with the Native Land Court, they were intended to be the main instruments of 'racial amalgamation'.

A distinctive feature of the New Zealand system was the requirement that Maori communities formally request schools and provide the land upon which they were to be built. It was believed, in official circles, that the enormous 'benefits of civilization' that the schools would provide should be recognized as such and actively sought by Maori communities. Maori needed to become willing participants in their own assimilation. By the early 1880s some 60 Maori communities had requested schools and the number of pupils enrolled continued to increase throughout the first half of the twentieth century. Native schools were finally amalgamated into the national public schools system in 1969. From 1909 onwards there were more Maori children attending schools in the public system, in which they were usually a minority, than there were in native schools.[9] Needless to say, assimilation was an unquestioned assumption in the national public schools where, like such schools in the United States and elsewhere, no provision at all was made for indigenous culture or language.

Native schools were supported by school committees, comprising local Maori parents and grandparents. Although these had no formal power – teachers were appointed centrally – in many communities their support was critical for the survival of the schools and their teachers, many of whom spoke little Maori. Prior to the introduction of compulsory schooling in 1894, school committees could and did withdraw support from bad teachers and discourage school attendance. Parents and grandparents retained considerable control over their children's attendance, removing them from school for important social events or when their labour was needed for planting or harvesting of crops. They retained full possession of their children. After the introduction of compulsory schooling, however, Maori community control over children became more difficult and schools began to take on the appearances of colonial Trojan horses. Rather than concealing soldiers in their bellies, native schools held Maori children captive in order to loosen and break their cultural bonds with their communities.

Schooling was entirely in English and in many (probably most) schools children were prohibited from speaking Maori, even in the playground. Accounts abound within Maori communities today of the frequent use of corporal punishment for speaking Maori and in many schools this was clearly a routine practice. Moreover, until the introduction of a few hours a week of Maori 'culture' in 1930, there was no place for Maori cultural knowledge or practices in the curriculum. The emphasis was upon teaching the 'three Rs' and providing manual and European domestic training. There was, therefore, a huge linguistic and cultural disjunction between home and school and this was experienced as such by many children. The children's coping strategies included not talking about their school experiences at home and withdrawing into themselves in the classroom. While the physical separation of children from their communities was not as marked as that in other settler nations, the linguistic and cultural separation promoted by native schools and general public schools in New Zealand has been just as enduring.

In the settler nations of Latin America the means of indigenous cultural separation varied between community-based schooling along the lines of that in Maori communities and residential schools like those in the United States. In Mexico, for example, urban residential schools were established for indigenous children in the 1920s and '30s. This system was intended both to separate children from their cultural communities and to facilitate their greater interaction with the wider Spanish-speaking population. During the second half of the 1930s, when Lázaro Cárdenas was president, boarding schools administered by the Department of Indigenous Affairs co-existed with community schools. All emphasized Spanish literacy combined with vocational training in agriculture and trades. Like Maori schools during the 1930s and '40s, token aspects of indigenous culture were introduced in order to strengthen support for schools and so assist the assimilation process. Since the 1960s there has been significant expansion in bilingual teaching in Mexico, with thousands of indigenous teachers now employed. The curriculum in many rural schools, however, still reflects the long tradition of assimilation in education and there remains considerable state resistance to further indigenization.

Most of the indigenous children whose school experiences we have been reviewing here have since become parents, grandparents and ancestors. The damage done to their lives through the trauma of alienation and separation cannot now be repaired. But what of their children and their children's children? Because assimilation was settlement, most no longer live with their communities on their ancestral land; many are not fluent in their ancestral languages and all are living the legacy of their forebears' dispossession. But as embodiments of this legacy, indigenous children have also become central to efforts to confront and overcome it. The transformation of indigenous dispossession into indigenous repossession, at the heart of indigenous politics in all settler states, includes the repossession of indigenous children, mainly through developments in indigenous schooling. I now turn to a discussion of some current projects of indigenous education and their place within the wider indigenous movements.

## The Repossession of Indigenous Children

If, as I have stressed, assimilation was settlement, requiring the dispossession of both land and children, then it follows that the most effective way for indigenous people to undo assimilation would be through the repossession of land and children. Given the violence that has been directed towards indigenous cultures by settler states, it could be argued that a taking back of land and children by force would be justified. In most cases, however, this would not be a practical option and it would certainly do nothing to enhance the moral case for indigenous rights. Instead, the repossession of land and children has had to be pursued through political and legal action within post-settler nations. Most concretely, it has meant the creation of spaces – literal and cultural – that are protected from the intrusion of state authorities and within which indigenous self-determination may be pursued.

I will argue in chapter Five that the creation of independent indigenous territories is of limited value for most peoples when they are economically marginal and where indigenous people have moved, or are moving, into urban areas. In such cases self-determination is largely illusory in that it is always heavily funded by post-settler states. He who pays the piper may not always call the tune, but if he doesn't like the music his payments may be reduced or cease altogether. Similarly, the establishment of indigenous schools as indigenous cultural spaces needs secure funding and this often means securing the continued support of the wider post-settler population. Among the important questions we need to ask are the following: Is it the case that indigenous schools can only become truly effective as a means for the repossession of children where intrusions by agents of the state are minimized? Or is it perhaps better to ensure the cooperation of post-settler states in funding indigenous education to the highest possible standards, even where this may mean less independence? Indigenous schools need actively to repossess children on behalf of their communities. But what if these communities are impoverished? What are the possibilities for indigenous control in such a context? And if such control becomes possible, to what ends should it be directed? In what follows I pursue some answers to these questions through a consideration of four very different examples of contemporary indigenous schooling within settler states: Zapatista schools in Mexico; Strelley 'mob' education in Australia; the Navaho Rough Rock School in the United States; and the predominantly urban kura kaupapa Maori schools in New Zealand.

In October 1992 Mayan protestors smashed to pieces the statue of the conquistador Diego de Mazariegos in the Chiapas city of San Cristóbal de las Casas. One observer later remarked that this event signalled the beginning of a 're-conquest in Chiapas'.[10] The fall of the statue symbolized a new phase in a struggle against five centuries of suffering and oppression that had seen Mayan communities in Mexico's southern most state ravaged by diseases (two-thirds of the population died in the mid-sixteenth century), slavery, forced food sales and massive land alienation. In the nineteenth century the expansion of haciendas by San Cristóbal elites transformed Mayan farmers into renters and migrant labourers living in a state of virtual servitude. The Mexican revolution of 1910 had brought little change; in 1936 the national Department of Indigenous Affairs declared that 'conditions of virtual slavery' still existed in Chiapas.[11]

From the 1950s onwards more intensive assimilation programmes were embarked upon by the government in an effort to produce Spanish-speaking peasant farmers. Settlement (in this case, indigenous re-settlement) and assimilation again went hand in hand as highland farmers, who had been displaced by haciendas, were encouraged to migrate to the Lacandón district and establish small farms (*ejidos*) for coffee and corn production. Bilingual schools staffed by inexperienced teachers, many of whom had not completed high school, were established to facilitate assimilation. In the 1960s and '70s many small farmers were further displaced into the jungle by cattle barons, and sporadic violence involving conflicts between farmers, ranchers and the government ensued in the 1980s.

Indigenous migrants to Lacandón came from a number of distinct language and cultural communities. However, their common cause in resisting state-backed ranchers encouraged them to recognize a common identity as poor, indigenous and Mayan. This new sense of collective identity found political expression in the Zapatista movement (Ejército Zapatista de Liberación Nacional, EZLN) that began forming in the 1980s. On 1 January 1994, a little over a year after the destruction of the statue in San Cristóbal, the Zapatista army, under the command of 'Subcomandante Marcos', entered the town and declared war on the Mexican government. A brief war and a brutal army occupation of Chiapas led to peace negotiations between Zapatistas and the government. Among the Zapatistas' main demands was indigenous control over adequately resourced and free education.

Following the 1994 fighting, Zapatistas expelled bilingual elementary school teachers from local schools and prohibited them from entering the villages in which they had been teaching. This was part of a wider attempt to evict agents of the state from Zapatista communities as a prelude to establishing structures that would ensure greater self-determination. To replace the expelled government teachers Zapatista villagers elected their own. While they were often chosen for their Spanish-speaking ability rather than their educational skills, the teachers were considered an improvement because they served only indigenous interests and were not compromised by the requirement to meet state objectives. The government sought to regain control over education through establishing an Indigenous Community Instructor Project to train these newly elected teachers. However, instead of bringing the teachers into the state fold, the government workshops provided an opportunity for the teachers to organize their own alternative forum, the Union of Teachers for New Education (UNEM).

UNEM members are drawn from more than 50 indigenous Chiapas communities in Lacandón and elsewhere in Chiapas. These communities have the highest illiteracy rates in Mexico, more than 50 per cent in some cases, compared to a rate of 6.5 per cent for Chiapas as a whole.[12] The union's aim is to create a new system of education that preserves indigenous cultures while at the same time providing knowledge relevant to the everyday lives of children. A crucial philosophical principle, broadly reflecting the teachings of Paulo Freire, is that teaching must combine theory and practice in order to change the world. In addition to reinterpreting Mayan history in order better to inform political practice, schools link classroom theory to the practicalities of local agriculture and lived indigenous culture.

The old boundaries between schools and communities are deliberately broken down while those between the state and schools are defended.

Central to the philosophy behind Zapatista schools is the concept of *Zapatismo* – the relating of all activities to the fight for freedom and equality. One teacher explained the approach as follows:

> The goal is to combine the system of Zapatismo (the struggle for freedom and equality of all people) with the ways of Mayan culture. The Zapatista approach to education is very compatible with the education philosophy of Paulo Freire [the Brazilian educator (1921–1997) known for his *Pedagogy of the Oppressed*, which intertwines learning with the struggle for social justice]. The teacher is not all knowing, but instead is both a teacher and a student. The teacher realizes the students will best understand concepts when the teacher and student work together. For example, at the school in Oventic there is a plan to teach animal husbandry by actually raising stock. The techniques used will combine the traditional methods that the students have learned from their communities with newer techniques learned from scientific advances.[13]

The school in Oventic, referred to above, is located within a free territory, or *aguascalientes*, one of a number that have been established by the Zapatistas in Chiapas. The term *aguascalientes* is derived from the name of the city in which Zapatista and other revolutionaries formulated, in 1914, a sweeping democratic programme for Mexico that is yet to be realized. Education within these democratic, non-military zones is part of a larger, indigenous public sphere that includes indigenous-controlled health services and cultural development. Unfortunately the zones are also under threat from the army, even though they pose no challenge to the political sovereignty of the Mexican state.

On the other side of the Pacific Ocean, Aboriginal communities are also resisting assimilation by breaking down boundaries between communities and schools and controlling state involvement. One such community is Strelley, in the Kimberley region of Western Australia. Although not as revolutionary as the Zapatistas, the Strelley 'mob' have a long history of struggle against injustice, including a strike for better wages in the 1940s that brought them into violent confrontation with squatters and police. The community has since strongly opposed the introduction of state-controlled education and in 1975 they began their own school to ensure that children would not become separated from Aboriginal social life.[14] Strelley leaders are proud that their school began an independent Aboriginal schools movement in Western Australia.

Central to the philosophy of the Strelley community is the necessity for everyone to adhere to 'the Law', a body of customs that are constantly being adapted to present circumstances. Outsiders, including white teachers, are expected to act in accordance with the Law and uphold the values of the community. They are given membership in a kin-group (moiety) and are required to interact with others in the community as kin-group members. This means observing gender-avoidance relations and contributing to the overall stability of the group. Classes are also divided along traditional moiety lines (two moieties, each with two subsections). The curriculum and teachers are controlled by an all-Aboriginal school board that ensures adherence to the Law.

Children in the beginner classes are mostly taught by Aboriginal teachers; older children usually have two teachers – one white, one Aboriginal. White teachers are employed specifically to develop literacy in English and numeracy skills while Aboriginal teachers are responsible for the wider curriculum, including literacy in local languages. Most recently the school has been reinforcing the speaking of the local Nyangumarta language through week-long camps and regular trips into the desert. Like the Chiapas schools, a significant portion of the curriculum is devoted to subjects closely related to the economic and social life of the community. In practice, this means linking the education process closely with the running and development of the community-owned cattle station. It also means that literacy classes discuss current issues facing the community and draw upon textual material produced within it.[15]

There can be no doubt that Chiapas schools in Mexico and Strelley education in Australia have developed real alternatives to the assimilation practices formerly pursued by their governments; children are no longer separated from their communities, while schooling, under indigenous control, has been tied to community development rather than community destruction. The communities have, to a large extent, succeeded in repossessing their land and their children. But we should be under no illusion that these communities will, as a consequence, become glowing examples of an indigenous cultural renaissance. Communities can build new schools but schools, no matter how independent they are, cannot build new communities.

Most indigenous Chiapas communities are desperately poor and very few remote Aboriginal communities are economically viable. While their schools can reclaim the children they cannot provide for most of them as future adults. Most remote Aboriginal communities consist largely of older people, mothers and children supported by welfare; the younger men between the ages of 20 and 40 have left in search of employment. Strelley leaders have become very concerned about the lack of employment for their children. The cattle station requires only a limited number of workers – and much of the work is now done with helicopters. Mining is looked to as a possible source of future employment, but prospects are limited at present. Young adults are also under-represented in remote Chiapas communities, where absolute poverty, rather than welfare dependency, is the overriding issue. Unless the establishment of indigenous-controlled rural schools is matched by significant economic improvements in the communities in which they are located, the repossession of their children will be a hollow victory for indigenous people. The North American Free

Trade Agreement has greatly increased economic pressures on already struggling communities, forcing many families to move to cities.

In both cases, it is not less state involvement but *better* state involvement in indigenous education that is required. Most importantly, there is a need for better teachers and greater support for teachers to encourage them to remain in indigenous communities. Many indigenous schools have very high staff turnovers; the teachers are too often young and inexperienced; and the academic expectations for the children are too low. Listen to Tania Major, an Aboriginal woman from Australia's Cape York:

> There is a huge gap between what we get in communities and what other kids get in cities. I got straight As at Kowanyama but when I got to Brisbane I was getting Cs and Ds. It really goes to show that there was something seriously wrong with the education system in our communities. One of the problems facing education in remote indigenous schools is that teachers tend to be just out of training and generally stay only a year or two. There was not one teacher who stayed for the whole of my nine years at school, even the principals . . . We need to review the curriculum in these communities because it is pitched at a very low level. I have had to draw the conclusion that Governments and educationalists see us as less than white people.

A criminology graduate, Tania Major was speaking here to the Prime Minister of Australia during a visit to her remote community, Kowanyama, where schools are largely under Aboriginal control. But Aboriginal control is one thing, securing adequate resources can be quite another.

Teresa McCarty concludes her deeply insightful history of the Navajo school at Rough Rock by highlighting this contradiction between educational control and economic marginality:

Can we create schools, as Paulo Freire (1993) envisioned, that are sites of social justice as well as creativity, competence and joy? Rough Rock has shown that school can be such a place, but with great difficulty and human cost. The larger question then remains: can such places of difference be sustained without denying equality of economic, social and educational opportunity to their inhabitants?[16]

When Rough Rock began in the mid-1960s it was widely regarded as a model for indigenous-controlled schooling – indeed, Strelley leaders drew inspiration from the early successes of this school. It was the first Indian school to teach in the indigenous language and it was at the forefront of developing indigenous teaching resources. By the mid-1990s, however, the school found itself in a state of crisis: it had become alienated from the Navajo community and became the target of protest action that split the community. The seeds of this crisis had been sown in the previous decade when the school struggled to survive in the face of massive state underfunding and inappropriate 'accountability' requirements. The school had not been able to defend its autonomy because it could not afford to do so. Since the school could not afford to defend its autonomy, it became a divisive force within the community.

Rough Rock school has since regained some of its former community support, but the dream of full indigenous control remains just that. The Rough Rock experience is by no means unique to rural indigenous schools. Where poverty prohibits self-funding, self-determination becomes a heroic struggle with little chance of ultimate success. Chronic underfunding and ongoing efforts by settler states to control curricula and administration become the norm rather than the exception. The contradiction between indigenous control and economic marginality poses a dilemma for many indigenous schools in rural areas: should they focus on integrating children into their impoverished communities or would they better assist their children (and, perhaps, ultimately their communities) by preparing them for successful and fulfilling lives as indigenous urban dwellers who maintain their ties with 'home'?

There are no easy answers here. Instead, recognition of this dilemma raises even more difficult questions, such as: what is the value of teaching children in their indigenous language if this language is little used beyond the community? The value may be an entirely practical one for communities where only an indigenous language is spoken, but the same pragmatic necessity does not exist in predominantly bilingual communities such as Rough Rock. A rationale for the promotion of teaching in the indigenous language in communities such as Rough Rock, and in many others in New Zealand, Australia, the United States and Canada, is that this language is endangered and with it the culture. But just as schools cannot create communities they cannot create language communities either. Certainly schools can contribute to linguistic and cultural revival, but we should not ask too much of them. In order for their distinct languages to flourish indigenous communities need, first, to have a strong sense of solidarity to which, as we have seen, indigenous schools may or may not contribute.

Urbanization everywhere undermines this solidarity and there is little or nothing that rural schools can do about this. Indigenous communities in the Brazilian Amazon stress that what they require from their schools is 'inter-cultural education', education that enables their children to move freely and successfully between different cultural worlds and that does not confine them to one. I am sure that this view is widely shared among indigenous parents in other post-settler nations. This is fine for rural people, but what of those living permanently in urban areas?

As I have already emphasized, most indigenous people are already urban dwellers and so the development of indigenous education programmes in urban centres will potentially have a greater impact on the futures of indigenous children than changes in rural education. Moreover, it could be argued that the cultural repossession of children is a much more urgent and pressing need for urban indigenous communities than for rural

ones; for rural people the concern is more often an inability to retain possession of their children, to hold on to their future generations. In the last
chapter I suggested that it is helpful to view the urbanization of indigenous
people as entailing, not a loss of indigenous culture, but a relocation of that
culture. Relocated culture is a transformed culture. There is always considerable interaction between rural and urban cultural forms – the movement of
people back and forth between urban and rural communities ensures that
both influence each other – but there is also divergence between them.
Indigenous urban schools are often more immediately confronted with this
cultural interaction and divergence than rural schools.

What, then, has the repossession of children meant for urban people?
Ironically, it has often meant the struggle to preserve rural-based cultures
and languages by teaching them to children who are thought to have lost
their culture. At least this is how indigenous schools, at the forefront of this
struggle, usually represent their task. What these schools are engaged in,
however, is never simply a reconnection of urban dwellers with rural kin
and ancestral land. Revalued and reinterpreted rural-based cultures also
inform new identities and underpin new forms of resistance to assimilation
in urban contexts. Urban schools make important contributions, therefore,
to new social movements that challenge the hegemony of settler nationhood and they often do so more effectively and more deeply than any
rural-based movement is able to. This, more than cultural preservation, is
what the repossession of indigenous children means in urban contexts.

While Zapatista schools have brought about significant changes to the
education of indigenous children in rural areas, an even greater challenge to
mestizo nationhood in Mexico will be urban schooling for indigenous children. As the Zapatistas feared, the introduction of the North American Free
Trade Agreement has gutted the rural economy and is rapidly emptying
rural Mayan villages. Cheap corn from the United States has flooded the
market, making it uneconomic for many indigenous people to plant local
corn on their small plots. Over the past ten years the numbers of urban

indigenous children has soared – around 40 per cent of Mexico's indigenous population is now urban, with more than half a million now living in the capital – and this has put pressure on the government to provide them with adequate bilingual schooling. In rural areas bilingual schooling has had little effect on the education of non-indigenous children but this is not the case in cities where classes are mixed. Non-indigenous parents complain that their children's progress is being held back by the need to accommodate indigenous languages and cultures, and they claim that training indigenous teachers and providing resources is too expensive.

The Mexican government is attempting to alleviate these fears by pouring extra resources into the bilingual schools. Computers are programmed in both Spanish and indigenous languages and additional teachers are being employed. Where there is only one indigenous language spoken by the majority of pupils these measures can be effective, but where several different languages are spoken schools face huge difficulties. One answer is greater indigenous control over urban schools, an approach that is being developed in New Zealand through the Kura Kaupapa Maori programme.

Kura Kaupapa Maori ('Schools based on a Maori Philosophy') are schools within the New Zealand state system that teach mainly in the Maori language and base their curriculum on Maori values. The first was established in 1985 and since then their numbers have grown to more than 60, catering for about 3 per cent of the total Maori school enrolments. Most schools (63 per cent) are officially classified as urban. In the early 1980s, as a political movement for Maori sovereignty was building, Maori pre-schools, termed kohanga reo (language nests), were established by Maori leaders, initially outside the state system. These subsequently gained government support and their numbers quickly expanded to more than 400 by 1985. Kura Kaupapa Maori were initially created as learning environments in which those children who had attended kohanga reo could continue to have their indigenous language skills and values affirmed and developed.

Kura Kaupapa Maori, while currently serving only a small minority of

Maori students, are regarded as critical for the survival of Maori language and culture in urban contexts. It is hoped that initial successes will have a snowballing effect and that, as the number of schools continues to increase, the number of Maori speakers will grow to a level where the survival of the language is assured. Recent reports suggest that this might be happening, although there is a long way to go yet. Most significantly, these schools affirm Maori identity and enhance self-esteem in ways that are not possible in the mainstream state system. In so doing, they not only reconnect children with their indigenous heritage, they also involve their parents and wider families in a collective project of cultural renewal and transformation. When indigenous culture becomes such a project it brings generations together in a common cause and begins to address the past separations that characterized settlement and the building of settler nations. Indigenous urban schools are able to realize their fullest potential in providing for their children's future only when they are at the centre of such projects.

No matter how successful indigenous schools are in providing spaces within post-settler nations for affirming and cultivating indigenous identities, schools do not create communities – rural or urban; nor can they fix what is wrong with them. They and their dedicated teachers cannot hope to overcome rural poverty, urban poverty or working-class alienation. Zapatista schools will only realize their full potential to the extent that the wider revolution succeeds in creating better economic and political futures for rural and urban people on the margins of global capitalism. Strelley 'mob' and Navajo schools, no matter how well they teach, cannot provide work for their students within their economically marginal communities. Their future, along with that of their communities, depends on the development of new economic and political linkages between rural and urban indigeneity. Kura Kaupapa Maori were established to further the cause of Maori self-determination or *tino rangatiratanga*, and their future expansion depends largely on the success of this movement in creating new identities and greater economic opportunities for their students.

# CHAPTER FIVE

# Indigenous Citizens

The tiny island of Niue, isolated in the Pacific Ocean to the north of New Zealand, has a local population of less than 1,500 people. It is the smallest country in the world. Between 1901 and 1974 the island was governed directly by New Zealand and its people are officially citizens of this post-settler state. When Niue became a self-governing territory in 1974, with its own parliament, premier, bureaucracy, flag and development plan, its people opted to retain their New Zealand citizenship rights. Niueans began leaving their island (or 'The Rock', as it is known locally) for New Zealand soon after self-government and the number residing in New Zealand is now around 20,000. The Government of Niue is propped up with millions of dollars of aid from New Zealand and the economy – if 1,500 people can be said to have an economy – is barely sustainable. Matters were made worse in January 2004 when a cyclone smashed many of the island's buildings, including houses, the hospital and tourist accommodation. Almost all the small businesses were left in ruins, and in the wake of the devastation some residents questioned whether it was worth rebuilding. One man who lost his house and most of his possessions commented: 'We're committed here because, A, we like it and, B, we've got so much money tied up here, but if you lost your house and you've got nothing else, why wouldn't you just leave? Just say "bugger it" and jump on a plane?'[1] More than this, some residents began to question the value of their national independence – perhaps it would be better to integrate with New Zealand?

Niue's political elite was, understandably, implacably opposed to the idea – the Premier labelled the mere suggestion of integration as 'immoral'. Besides, he said, 'If we integrated with New Zealand, just imagine the kinds of things we would need with the education system, the health system, for it to be equal. The infrastructure has to be the same if we say we should be integrated.'[2] But for others this was precisely the reason they wanted integration. One local villager who lost her house, fruit trees and taro crops said that she, like many others, wanted to stay on Niue, but only if she could get a good education for her four children. Only by becoming part of New Zealand would this be guaranteed, she thought.

Nunavut, a frozen land of snow and ice in northern Canada, is about as far away from tropical Niue as you can get. But, like Niue, Nanavut is also a self-governing territory with its own premier, legislative assembly and flag. Also like Niue, most of its budget is provided by the post-settler state that formerly ruled the territory directly. The majority of the 29,000 residents of Nunavut are Inuit who live in isolated communities and whose main sources of livelihood are hunting and trapping. However, many people are also highly dependent upon the government for housing (about half the houses are maintained by the government), the unemployment rate is around 20 per cent, and almost a third of the population is supported by welfare payments. With a birth rate that is twice the Canadian average there are increasing pressures on the government to provide new housing and more classrooms. Providing employment opportunities for teenagers, who now comprise almost 40 per cent of the population, will be a massive challenge in the near future. Unless new jobs can be created many young people will move south. There is potential for jobs and greater economic independence through the development of gold and diamond mining, tourism and fisheries management, but Nunavut will continue to rely heavily upon grants from the Canadian Federal Government well into the foreseeable future.

The situations of Niue and Nunavut illustrate very clearly the core paradox of indigenous sovereignty: continued political and cultural independence is dependent upon the economic and political support of post-settler states. The question that these examples pose is: can such dependent independence be accurately described as indigenous sovereignty? Of course, the sovereignty of every nation is limited by the sovereignty of other nations, but indigenous sovereignty in these cases is directly funded by another nation and is, in part at least, an expression of that other nation's political will. The discursive field within which this 'will to fund autonomy' is formed includes a moral argument for cultural nationalism and culturally based citizenship. However, when the virtues of cultural nationalism become less obvious and its oppressive potential more apparent – and this is already happening – the post-settler will to fund cultural autonomy may weaken.

The term 'indigenous citizen' is meaningless until we specify the imagined political community of which indigenous people claim membership and/or the political community that claims them as members. The world can hardly be described as a single political community, no matter how strongly we hold to the idea of a common humanity, and so citizenship cannot be usefully conceived of at this level. Below this level, you cannot be a citizen of the Labour Party, London or Amnesty International. Citizenship has historically been connected intimately to both statehood and nationhood. As a regime deployed most often by states, it defines the boundaries and conditions of membership in national communities. Furthermore, it assumes a formal, reciprocal recognition of national belonging – citizens are expected to declare their allegiance to the nation and, in return, the nation confers legitimacy upon some, but not all claims to membership; crucially, it has the power to exclude those whom it considers do not belong.

Regimes of citizenship deployed by nation-states have rarely been uncontested, however. There are now challenges being mounted from above and below. The formation of new political communities such as the EU has entailed new ways of regulating the relations between states, markets and nations. Indigenous peoples, many of whom have never been fully included in citizenship regimes, now seek greater self-determination outside or within them. In this chapter I argue that if indigenous citizenship is to have a future then it will need to draw its moral legitimacy, at least initially, from a universal discourse that upholds the idea of participatory democracy rather than one that upholds the notion of cultural autonomy.

Colonization was always a conditional extension of the boundaries of the colonizing nation to include the indigenous inhabitants of the settler states. In some states, such as New Zealand and the United States, these conditions included individual property ownership. In addition, indigenous belonging within settler nations frequently required the renouncing of allegiances to indigenous culture as a source of distinctive identity. In Canada, people had to renounce their membership of reserve bands in order to enter the settler nation. In the United States, following the passing of the Dawes Act in 1887, those Indians issued with allotments were eligible for American citizenship once they had formally renounced their Indian identity. A government representative read from the following script:

> FOR MEN: (Read White name) what is your Indian name? (gives Indian name)
>
> (Indian name), I hand you a bow and arrow. Take this bow and arrow and shoot the arrow. (Shoots arrow.)
>
> (Indian name), you have shot your last arrow. That means that you are no longer to live the life of an Indian. You are from this day forward to live the life of a white man. But you may keep the arrow, it will be to you a symbol of your noble race and the pride you feel that you come from the first of all Americans. (White name), take

in your hands this plough. (Takes plough.) This act means that you have chosen to live the life of the white man – and the white man lives by work. From the earth we all must get our living and the earth will not yield unless man pours the sweat of his brow. Only by work do we gain a right to land and enjoyment of life.

The government representative then gave the candidate a purse, symbolizing thrift, and a flag. He was then asked to repeat the following oath:

> For as much as the President has said that I am worthy to be a citizen of the United States, I now promise to this flag that I will give my hands, my head, and my heart to the doing of all that will make me a true American citizen.

The flipside of formal admittance was formal exclusion. In Australia, for example, Aboriginal people were specifically excluded from citizenship at the time of federation in 1901. Prior to federation, Aboriginal people were British subjects and men were legally entitled to vote in four of the six self-governing Australian states. However, with the passing of the Commonwealth of Australia Constitution Act in 1900 and the Commonwealth Franchise Act in 1902, all Aboriginal people were deemed to be outside the Australian nation and ineligible for membership. The Constitution Act stipulated that Aboriginal people should not be counted in any official census and the Franchise Act stated that 'No Aboriginal native of Australia, Asia, Africa or the Islands of the Pacific except New Zealand shall be entitled to have his name on the electoral roll'. It would not be until 1967 that, following a nation-wide referendum, members of the Australian nation formally agreed to allow Aboriginal people to join their political community through the repeal of the offending sections of the Commonwealth Act. The exclusion clause of the Franchise Act had been repealed in 1962.

Alcida Ramos writes that Brazilian citizenship offers three legal possibilities: Brazilian, foreigner or Indian. In practice, if not in law, a parallel situation exists in all post-settler nations. In Brazil, 'The foreigner may become a citizen by a legal bureaucratic act revealingly named naturalization. Indians cannot become naturalized, for they are already "naturals of the land". What they can do is be "emancipated", that is, relieved of their special status.'[3]

Such 'emancipation', which was proposed by the Brazilian state in the mid-1970s, was, in truth, an attempt to remove indigenous land rights and fully integrate them as individuals into the Brazilian nation. Accordingly it met with the same hostile response from indigenous leaders that had followed the earlier release, by the Canadian government, of its 1969 White Paper on Indian Policy. Like Brazil's 'emancipation' decree, this White Paper sought to confer full citizenship rights upon Indians through the elimination of Indian status and all special rights associated with it. Indians would join existing members of the settler nation as 'equals'; reserve resources would become individualized; and the Department of Indian Affairs would be phased out.

Indigenous leaders were eventually able to block both of these proposals. International opinion by the late 1970s was moving towards the view that, if indigenous people were to be admitted as full citizens of settler nations, they should not have to give up their cultural identity as a precondition of acceptance. In addition, in both Brazil and Canada the prospect of forced citizenship galvanized indigenous groups into political action: a massive show of collective opposition forced the Canadian government to abandon its White Paper in 1971, and the Union of Indian Nations formed in Brazil two years after the emancipation decree. Ramos points out that Indians would have lost democratic protections for their distinctive ways of life if they had been legally transformed into 'ordinary' Brazilian citizens. Polygamy, infanticide, nakedness, the use of hallucinogens, some mortuary rites and modes of social control would have automatically become illegal, since such 'un-Brazilian' practices would no longer have official protection.[4] The same may have applied in Canada. But the most destructive effect of this individualized emancipation would have been the official severance of the distinctive relationships between indigenous groups and their land.

Individualized emancipation is by no means a forgotten 1970s option. As I write this chapter, Don Brash, the leader of New Zealand's main opposition National Party, proposes in a 'state of the nation' address to emancipate Maori by abolishing legal recognition of Maori interests. The recognition of indigenous rights is, in his view, creating a form of separatism that is in contradiction to the notion that New Zealanders should be treated as 'one people'. If he were a Maori, he says, he would view legislation that specifically required consultation with Maori, in addition to consultation with the wider community, as condescending because it assumes Maori are not part of that wider community. Maori need to be liberated from the shackles of separatism in order to become New Zealand citizens with the same rights as all other citizens. While some members of the right-wing establishment consider the leader's speech bold and timely, Maori members of the National Party are moving quickly to distance themselves from it. One high-profile Maori member, Hekia Parata, writes that she is now 'ashamed' to have stood for the party at the last election. In a feature article in the local paper, she critiques the central assumptions of the speech and proposes an alternative position: 'The core flaw is the conflation of the dual identities of Maori as an ethnic citizen of New Zealand and Maori as an indigenous member of a particular tribal group . . . It is not Maori citizens who have any customary rights or claims to title. It is specific *iwi* [tribes].'[5]

For Parata, ethnic citizenship is distinct from indigenous tribal membership. Ethnic citizenship requires appropriate cultural policies while tribal identity, tied to specific geographical locations, requires policies that address indigenous rights which, in New Zealand, are embodied in the Treaty of Waitangi. The creation of a single, homogenous citizenship would address neither cultural nor tribal concerns.

Multicultural policies and the notion of cultural citizenship have been elaborated in most settler states to deal with the recognition of cultural differences within nations, which are now imagined as culturally diverse political communities. While these concepts have been generally helpful for indigenous people in South America struggling against mestizo nationalisms and for migrant minorities elsewhere struggling against settler nationalisms, they do not address the issue of how to include indigenous people as territorial communities within settler nations. Indigenous people are culturally distinct – but they are also territorially distinct. When the territory of an indigenous group lies within that claimed by the settler nation – and this is invariably the case unless the indigenous territory lies across the borders of two or more nations – then the recognition of a culturally distinct indigenous citizenship must also entail the recognition of a distinctive indigenous space. Not to do so would be to treat indigenous people as if they were simply another minority, in the same position *vis-à-vis* the settler majority as later migrant groups. If, within this recognized indigenous space, indigenous people were free to be culturally different, then the recognition of a culturally distinct indigenous citizenship would come very close to an acceptance that indigenous people possess a dual nationality.

To date, no settler nation has officially gone this far, but dual nationality is not really such a radical notion. After all, it is common for countries to allow their citizens to hold more than one passport – British citizens may also be citizens of Australia or New Zealand, for example. Why not allow indigenous people to be citizens of a post-settler nation and an indigenous nation simultaneously? The Nunavut and Niuean cases approximate dual nationality, although in neither instance do the people carry two passports. But why stop at dual citizenship? Why not go all the way and give indigenous people the choice of relinquishing their citizenship in the post-settler nation in favour of a recognized citizenship within an indigenous nation?

This latter course of action has been seriously proposed for American Indians by Professor Robert Porter.[6] Porter would like to see what he terms 'a modified repeal' of the Indian Citizenship Act 1924, by which United States citizenship was forced upon about a third of the American Indian population – most had already become citizens through the allotment process, treaty provisions, birth and other means. Despite the fact that many indigenous Americans were given no choice in relation to American citizenship in 1924, Porter acknowledges that most would now oppose any move to revoke it unilaterally. Instead, a 'Choice of Citizenship Act' should be passed containing a provision stating that those Indians who choose to remain American citizens will no longer be recognized under Federal law as citizens of an indigenous nation – they will become just like any other American citizen. For those who choose not to retain their American citizenship and instead give their sole allegiance to an Indian nation, Porter sees both costs and benefits. They would be unable to vote or stand for political office in the United States and they would be ineligible for public education and welfare services as of right. But, on the other hand, they would not be required to serve in the US military or pay US taxes. Porter leaves open the question of whether non-US Indians would be able to work in the United States without permission.

Porter admits that the number of people willing to give up American citizenship would be a small percentage of the Indian population, given that only a half to two-thirds are tribal members and that many of these would be unwilling to make the necessary initial sacrifices. He does not believe, however, that those people with a desire for self-determination should be prevented from reclaiming their full indigenous nationhood by the majority who, largely because they have been too fully assimilated, want to maintain the status quo.

While, on the face of it, Porter's proposals seem radical, on closer inspection they come alarmingly close to the views of Australians and Canadians who maintained that indigenous people had only two options: to remain (and die) as full Aborigines and Indians on reserves or to give up their indigenous identities and become 'ordinary' assimilated Australians or Canadians. Both these views and Porter's exhibit the oppressive authenticity that I criticized in chapter Two. Indeed, one could easily imagine the right-wing leader of New Zealand's National Party modifying his proposals in line with Porter's: Maori should be given the choice to abandon all special rights and become 'ordinary' New Zealand citizens or join a tribe and lose these rights anyway.

In practice, Porter's indigenous nations, with their self-selected groups of committed indigenous citizens, would not be very different from Niue or Nunavut – except that his citizens would carry their own indigenous passports. Their geographic and economic marginality would remain, and so too would such pressing issues as high unemployment, relatively low educational levels and poor health. Reserves and marginal environments are rarely a sufficient territorial base upon which to build exclusive indigenous nations. Almost all indigenous leaders recognize this; rather than full sovereignty, most seek cultural and political autonomy within the larger, more economically secure post-settler nations. It is quite clear that most indigenous leaders, and certainly most indigenous people, would favour a form of dual citizenship over an exclusive indigenous citizenship that positioned them outside the post-settler nation. The term 'indigenous sovereignty', widely used by indigenous leaders in international political discourse, is often, therefore, quite ambiguous.

The ambiguity and Eurocentricity of the notion of state sovereignty has led some indigenous commentators to question its appropriateness as a goal for indigenous peoples. Dr Taiaiake Alfred, a Mohawk and Director of the Indigenous Governance Programme at Canada's University of Victoria, has argued:

> The next phase of scholarship and activism . . . will need to transcend the mentality that supports the colonization of indigenous nations, beginning with the rejection of the term and notion of indigenous 'sovereignty' . . . Sovereignty itself implies a set of values and objectives that put it in direct opposition to the values and objectives found in most traditional indigenous philosophies. Non-

indigenous politicians recognize the inherent weakness of a position that asserts a sovereign right for peoples who do not have the cultural frame and institutional capacity to defend or sustain it.[7]

Instead, Alfred argues, indigenous people need to detach the notion of sovereignty from its legal, western roots and transform it into a doctrine that more closely conforms to traditional values. Among these values are notions of sharing and a kinship or caretaker relationship to the land rather than one of territorial control and domination. Alfred writes that, prior to colonization, indigenous people lived in 'sovereignty-free regimes of conscience and justice that allowed for the harmonious coexistence of humans and nature for hundreds of generations'. He concludes that a post-imperial world will need to return to the values that underpinned these regimes rather than perpetuate western models of sovereign domination and control.[8]

We can extend Alfred's case against the Eurocentric nature of sovereignty to the notions of citizenship and universal human rights: these concepts, too, are deeply rooted western notions of the individual. Despite the fact that all three notions are Eurocentric, there is a profound tension between them in western political thought – nations legitimize themselves with reference to a discourse on universal human rights while at the same time negating, in their very existence, the common humanity they profess; both individual citizens and the nations to which they belong are said to possess sovereignty and have the right to self-determination. Indigenous citizenship, like indigenous sovereignty, carries with it this baggage of ambiguity and contradiction. Alfred's transformed view of sovereignty also requires a similarly transformed notion of citizenship – one that reflects non-individualistic membership in tribal communities and collective relationships with land and the environment. In other words, indigenous citizenship becomes a type of territorial kinship.

The problem with equating indigenous citizenship and territorial kinship is, as we saw in chapter Three, that most indigenous people are urban. Many relocated indigenous people do, of course, maintain strong links with 'home' communities and so a case can be made for regarding indigenous citizenship as an historically rural identity that is being maintained and transformed in urban contexts. But when 'sovereignty' and self-determination are centred on reserves, the participation of urban people in indigenous political life is severely limited. For them, it is often not self-determination but, instead, other-determination, where the 'other' belongs to a government-supported, rural leadership that makes little attempt to involve urban people fully in decision-making processes. Governments find it easier not to involve urban people fully, too, preferring to fund 'reserve sovereignty' in the hope that rural leaders will somehow deal with the messier reality of transitory and relocated lives.

When governments and indigenous leaders propose that the relationship between post-settler nations and indigenous people should be conceived as that of 'nation-to-nation', they are by no means proposing a relationship of the same order that exists between nations within the United Nations. To equate the relationship between Canada and Nunavut with the relationship between Canada and the United States is to misrepresent fundamentally the true nature of indigenous sovereignty. On the one hand we have a democratic, multicultural nation of individual citizens whose defended territory encompasses that of the indigenous people, while on the other hand we have a relatively small and culturally distinct group of people connected through kinship and inhabiting a marginal territory within the larger national space. And the concept of 'nation-to-nation' becomes even less accurate when it describes relationships between states and indigenous peoples whose leadership is based on reserves or in small rural communities. This 'nation-to-nation' model is deeply Eurocentric in that it assumes indigenous nations should exist, first, on a map; that nations control territories through states (or their equivalent) and that these 'states' embody the political will of the inhabitants of the mapped territories.

Both this 'nation-to nation' model and Alfred's territorial kinship reinforce a marginalized indigeneity, a 'reserve sovereignty' that is all too often founded upon poverty and welfare dependency. In such circumstances, meaningful self-determination is impossible. Welfare dependency is having devastating effects on indigenous communities, especially upon men, many of whom have come to see themselves as making no real economic contribution to their families. This impacts, in turn, upon the women and children who suffer from domestic violence and the effects of male drinking. In an address to the Prime Minister of Australia, Tania Major, the young woman from the remote Cape York region we met earlier, eloquently described the social devastation of her people:

> In less than 60 years the people of my tribe have gone from being an independent nation to cultural prisoners to welfare recipients. Is it any wonder that there are so many problems facing indigenous Australians today? Prime Minister, I want you to gain a brief picture of the life of young people in our communities. When I was growing up in Kowanyama there were 15 people in my class. Today I am the only one that has gone to university, let alone finished secondary education. I'm also the only girl in my class who did not have a child at 15. Of the boys in my class seven have been incarcerated, two for murder, rape and assault. Of the 15 there are only three of us who are not alcoholics. And, Prime Minister, one of the saddest things I must report to you is that four of my class mates have already committed suicide.[9]

Also reinforced through 'nation-to-nation' thinking is the idea that indigenous people are at their most authentic when they belong to self-administered marginal communities. Outside these indigenous 'nations' they are migrants, displaced people who don't fully belong as citizens of the post-settler nation. A cynic might argue that because Canada could not provide a secure place for Inuit within its nation, a place where Inuit identity could flourish, it welcomed the opportunity to remove Inuit from the Canadian nation. It is likewise for Indian 'nations' in the United States and many self-administered communities and tribes elsewhere. 'Nation-to nation' models reinforce a separation between those who wish to remain on the land and those who don't. A treaty negotiated between the Canadian government and the Nisga'a 'nation' (half of whom are urban), for example, ensures that political control over land and all money resides with those who remain on the land and 'outside' the Canadian nation. Similar provisions are included in many self-administration models in place elsewhere.

Furthermore, while many indigenous leaders and rural people are passionate advocates for a way of life that is tied to the land – their land and the land of their ancestors – most indigenous people don't want to be confined to reserves and rural communities, usually for very good reasons. As one urban Aboriginal from Canada put it: 'The reserves are only good for some people. The "have nots" from the reserve end up in cities – treated like second class citizens in our own communities. All the reserves are like this – under self-government the rich get rich and the poor get poorer.'[10]

The problem is compounded when indigenous nationalism becomes indigenous cultural nationalism – when reserve sovereignty is predicated upon cultural allegiance. Typically the 'culture' to which this allegiance is owed is one rooted in rural traditions upheld by politically conservative men.

Indigenous people do not belong to 'nations within' and nor do they seek to belong to 'nations without'. Most indigenous people seek full indigenous citizenship *within* post-settler nations – secession is rarely a political objective – but in doing so they seek recognition as distinct 'peoples', as first 'peoples'. The term 'people' is controversial in international law because it is tied to rights of self-determination. The International Covenant on Civil and Political Rights and the International Covenant on Economic, Social and Cultural Rights have enshrined the principle that 'all peoples' have the right to self-determination. The most controversial article of the United Nations Draft Declaration on the Rights of Indigenous Peoples, Article 3, seeks to emphasize that indigenous peoples are included in the term 'all peoples'. It does this by reproducing the wording of Article 1, Paragraph 1, of both International Covenants, except that the words 'All peoples' in the first sentence is replaced by 'Indigenous peoples'. Article 3, therefore, reads as follows: 'Indigenous peoples have the right to self-determination. By virtue of that right they freely determine their political status and freely pursue their economic, social and cultural development.'

The wording of this Article is, not surprisingly, unacceptable to most states because they fear that its adoption would undermine both their internal stability and the stability of the international order. Many governments want to define 'self-determination' as 'self-government', thus mandating a devolution of some state powers to indigenous leaders, a situation that already exists in many countries. Others go further and also oppose the use of the term 'indigenous peoples', seeking to have it replaced by the more general term 'indigenous people' or the more neutral 'indigenous populations'.

One of the underlying ambiguities of the international legal struggle between indigenous leaders and governments is that, in practice, most indigenous leaders do not seek the same 'self-determination' that states wish to uphold for their nations. For states the crucial issue is territorial integrity; for indigenous leaders it is political and cultural autonomy within states. It is quite possible for these two notions of self-determination to coexist: the creation of Nunavut is clear evidence that they are by no means mutually exclusive. Because Nunavut is both a territory *within* Canada and an expression of Inuit desire for political and cultural autonomy, it satisfies Canada's concern to maintain its territorial integrity as well as providing for Inuit self-determination. Reserves and reservations also do this to a lesser extent, as do many other forms of devolution practised in South America, Australia and New Zealand. The pressing question, therefore, is not how indigenous peoples can achieve the same level or type of self-determination that is upheld by states but how they should *extend* and transform the indigenous self-determination that already exists within these states.

The answers to this question will not be found in international legal forums and United Nations talk-fests, where arguments over the meaning of the terms 'indigenous' and 'people' take precedence over the realities of political power and accommodation. There is little or no recognition within these forums of the distinctiveness of the self-determination being pursued by indigenous peoples within settler states in relation to that being pursued by tribal peoples in Third World states. This includes negotiations with post-settler governments around a form of citizenship that recognizes both historical precedence (indigenous peoples were there first) and a contemporary context that includes intermarriage and urbanization.

Indigenous cultural nationalism, such as that pursued by Nunavut, and models advocated by Porter and Alfred are just some of the distinctive ways in which self-determination might be extended and transformed within post-settler states. Others include the Sami Parliament of Finland (Sametinget) and the Kuna General Congress of Panama. Both of these political bodies are legally mandated to implement cultural autonomy within defined homelands. The Finnish Sami Act of 1996 obliges the state to 'negotiate' with the Parliament on matters such as community planning, land management and resource conservation, and legislation affecting 'traditional' Sami practices and the teaching of Sami language in schools. The Kuna General Congress, which has been in place since 1953, is presided over by grand chiefs representing different regions of the Kuna territory, covering some forty small islands and part of the mainland along the Caribbean coast. The Congress includes representatives from most local communities, including urban ones.

All of these models are, however, political expressions of a territorially based cultural nationalism and so they cannot effectively address a situation in which culturally diverse indigenous peoples are spread widely throughout a country or within regions of a country. There is no doubt that this latter scenario will increasingly become the reality for most indigenous people where it hasn't done so already. In countries such as New Zealand, Mexico, Bolivia and Ecuador, where there is no history of reserve confinement, these models of 'reserve sovereignty' make little or no sense. Even where there has been a history of reserves or territorial marginality we need to ask if reserve sovereignty and 'nation-to-nation' dependency are really what most indigenous people want for themselves and their children? Is this the best they can hope for politically and economically? I am sure that the answer to both of these questions will often be 'no'. But I am equally certain that there is no single model of indigenous citizenship that will be suitable for all post-settler states.

Factors that influence the effectiveness and legitimacy of any model of indigenous citizenship include, at a minimum, the following: the size of the indigenous population relative to other groups within the post-settler nation; the distribution of the indigenous population between rural and urban locations and throughout the state's territory in general; and the extent of cultural diversity within the indigenous population. One could, I suppose, draw up a grid with these variables represented on it and plot the different possible models of self-determination in relation to them, but such an elaborate mathematical game is not really necessary. In reality, most indigenous peoples are either small minorities relative to other groups or they constitute relatively large, but geographically distinct populations. Where indigenous peoples are small minorities, further variation can be minimally represented in terms of a simple two-by-two matrix as follows:

|  | Cultural Diversity | |
| --- | --- | --- |
|  | HIGH | LOW |
| Distribution Restricted | 1 | 2 |
| Distribution Wide | 3 | 4 |

Examples of variation 1 would include the Amazonian Indians of Brazil; variation 2 is represented by the Inuit of Nunavut; variation 3 is represented by Native Americans in the United States; and examples of variation 4 include the Maori of New Zealand and Native Hawai'ians within Hawai'i. The second main group of indigenous peoples, not represented in this matrix, are those who comprise a relatively large proportion of the population of a post-settler state and who are concentrated in particular regions of these states. Examples include the highland peoples of Ecuador, Bolivia and Peru and the indigenous peoples of Mayan origin in Mexico.

This is, as I have said, very much a minimalist representation of just a few dimensions that influence the appropriateness of different models of indigenous citizenship. Equally significant, of course, are the formal political structures of the post-settler states. Brazil, Mexico, Canada, the United States, New Zealand and Australia are, constitutionally, very different political communities. If the Inuit had been living in Brazil the creation of a tropical Nunavut would not have had the model of provincial autonomy, characteristic of Canada, to emulate. If the culturally diverse Amazonian Indian communities had inhabited northern Canada, Nunavut would not have been envisaged. If the New Zealand Maori had been living in the United States the ideas of reservations and distinct 'nations' would have made less political sense. In addition to the political structures of states, the nature of the traditional and post-traditional indigenous polities significantly influence the ways in which self-determination might be extended.

The main point I am making, then, is that any particular model of indigenous citizenship is always going to have limited applicability beyond the post-settler context in which it is formulated. The Nunavut solution to the extension of Inuit self-determination within Canada might have some applicability in Northern Australia (both are variation 2 contexts in the figure above), but it will have more limited applicability elsewhere. The same is true for all the diverse ways in which indigenous people have sought, and are seeking, to extend their self-determination within post-settler states. Irrespective of the model of indigenous citizenship that is adopted, however, the crucial question must be how effective it is in enhancing or ensuring the political participation and recognition of indigenous peoples, *as indigenous peoples*, within post-settler states.

The creation of a distinct indigenous territory may have achieved this for the Inuit, but elsewhere it may lead to a reduced participation by indigenous people in post-settler democracy. By confining and institution-alizing indigenous political participation within 'homelands', the larger post-settler nation is able to redefine itself as comprising two distinct political communities, one of which now has less need to recognize indigenous voices and accommodate indigenous views. When this political external-ization of indigenous people coincides with economic marginalization, as it often does, then indigenous participation in the post-settler state rarely takes place on indigenous terms. And it goes without saying that such models do not give indigenous people an enhanced ability to change the governments of their post-settler states.

If cultural nationalism, expressed through territorial separation, is not a viable option for extending the self-determination of many, perhaps most, indigenous peoples, what practical options are left? Let us briefly consider two very different alternative models – Zapatista indigenism and the creation of separate Maori parliamentary seats in New Zealand. I am not suggesting that either of these models is directly exportable for the reasons just presented, but, because both are attempts to provide for a higher level of democratic participation by indigenous peoples as indigenous peoples within post-settler democracies, they provide a valuable contrast to the examples of nationalist separatism discussed so far. If, as I argue, the future of indigenous citizenship is going to depend more on the political recogni-tion and empowerment of indigenous peoples as distinctive actors within post-settler democracies than on the political recognition of distinct indige-nous territories, then the success or otherwise of Zapatista indigenism and the Maori seats will be of wide significance for indigenous peoples – wider, perhaps, than the Nunavut experiment.

Mexico, like Brazil, Ecuador and Bolivia, has declared itself to be a pluri-ethnic state. Indeed, in the late 1980s it was the first country in Latin America to ratify the ILO Convention 169 recognizing indigenous rights.

But what does this mean in practice for regions within Mexico with relatively large indigenous populations? Does it mean a rethinking of the formal political structures to enable greater political participation by indigenous people as regional representatives? Does it mean devolution of state power to these regions? Zapatista leaders argue strongly that it does and have been struggling for ten years to convince a reluctant Mexican government that it has to back up its pluri-ethnic rhetoric with real political changes.

As we saw in the last chapter, indigenous rights were placed firmly on the Mexican national agenda in 1994 by the Zapatista National Liberation Army (Ejército Zapatista de Liberación Nacional, EZLN). The rebellion was timed to coincide with the coming into effect of the North American Free Trade Agreement (NAFTA). After sixteen days of fighting, Zapatista leaders and the government agreed to negotiate over long-standing economic and political concerns; the initial Zapatista communiqué listed 'work, land, housing, food, health care, education, independence, freedom, democracy, justice and peace'. It is significant that at this stage there was no specific mention of indigenous rights – these were viewed as part of wider demands for democracy, freedom and justice. The support base for the Zapatistas came overwhelmingly from indigenous people, however, and as the political programme began to be formulated through local meetings and a National Indigenous Forum in January 1996 indigenous rights became a key demand. But this was not a cultural nationalist movement. Represented at the forum were 178 indigenous organizations including representatives from 36 different cultural groups. While the leaders of these groups wanted greater recognition of their distinct cultures in terms of education, health and political process, this was to be achieved through increased autonomy and democracy at the regional level rather than through the recognition of culturally defined nations.

These objectives are reflected in the San Andrés Accords signed by the Zapatistas and the government a month later. 'Document Two' of the Accords states that the parties commit themselves to:

1. The creation of a new legal framework that establishes a new relationship between *pueblos indigenas* and the state based on their right to self-determination and the legal, political, social, economic and cultural rights associated with it. The new constitutional dispositions must include a framework of autonomy.

2. This legal framework must be built on the recognition of the self-determination of *pueblos indigenas*, which are those that, having historical continuity with societies that predated the imposition of the colonial regime, maintain their own identities, are aware of them, and possess the will to preserve them . . . The exercise of autonomy of *pueblos indigenas* will contribute to the *unity and democratization of national life and strengthen the country's sovereignty* [emphasis added].[11]

The term *pueblos indigenas*, which appears throughout the Spanish version of the Accords, is ambiguous. Among the meanings of *pueblo* are 'town', 'community' and 'people'. The extension of indigenous self-determination in Mexico was, therefore, envisaged as entailing the recognition of a wide range of different cultural groups and historical communities. Most crucially, this legal recognition was envisaged as contributing to the democratization and sovereignty of the larger post-settler nation.

Unfortunately, the Mexican government has not made good its promises in the Accords. A constitutional change in 2001 acknowledged Indian peoples but no specific measures to increase indigenous autonomy have been put in place. As a result of what is widely viewed as a betrayal by the government, the Zapatistas led a massive demonstration by more than 20,000 people in the centre of San Cristóbal de las Casas in 2003. It remains to be seen whether the indigenous democratization envisaged by the Zapatistas will gain formal constitutional support.

The Zapatista demands are about regional and cultural autonomy rather than secession. However, the political changes required to implement them would be extensive, affecting both central and local governance. Increased participation in national life for indigenous Mexicans would mean not only new structures to ensure greater local autonomy, but also new linkages between autonomous *pueblos* and the centre. This would, in turn, put increased pressures on central government to devolve greater resources to *pueblos*, to ensure that this is done fairly, and to ensure that those receiving the resources are legitimate representatives of their people. All of this has the potential to transform Mexican political life deeply and bring about a reassessment of the values upon which the nation is founded. It represents a vision of a new kind of democracy within which indigenous cultures have greater security, protected from assimilation and fostered within a more inclusive political culture.

This is not a vision that impresses the supporters of NAFTA. For them, less political autonomy for local producers means a weaker national lobby and more likelihood that 'the market' will determine prices free from political interference. The seemingly restricted local demands for autonomous *pueblos* have, therefore, far-reaching international significance. Zapatista leaders were, of course, always well aware of this: the potential for NAFTA to increase rural poverty has been a principal cause of protest since the earliest days of the uprising. They are also well aware that centralized monetarist governments are absolutely critical for the growth of global capitalism, maintaining commodity and labour flows in the interests of the market. Movements for regional autonomy and increased democracy such as that initiated by the Zapatistas not only reduce the ability of governments to create and maintain free markets in the interest of trans-national capital, but they also redefine citizenship, indigenous and non-indigenous, as an identity in conflict with global capitalism.

While the Zapatista movement is not an expression of cultural nationalism, it does assume a degree of territorial separation or regionalism. A controversial model of indigenous citizenship that assumes neither cultural nationalism nor territorial separation is one in which indigenous people have special voting rights; indigenous citizens are given the option of voting in indigenous electorates and electing indigenous representatives to sit in the national parliament. New Zealand has operated under this system since 1867. Before this date, only Maori with individual freehold title to land were able to vote. The creation of Maori electorates in 1867 was accompanied by an extension of voting rights to all Maori males over 21 years of age. This was by no means a genuine attempt by settlers to include indigenous people fully in the political system, however, since Maori were only allocated four of the 76 seats in Parliament – had the number of seats been calculated on a per capita basis Maori would have been entitled to at least fourteen seats. The number of Maori seats remained at four for the next 130 years, providing Maori with very little parliamentary power as indigenous citizens. Furthermore, for most of the twentieth century the strong allegiance of Maori MPs to one party significantly reduced their influence in Parliament. Around half of the Maori voters, disillusioned with a system that only served to constrain their influence, have switched from the Maori electoral roll to the general electoral roll during the last few decades.

In 1996, however, a new electoral system of proportional representation was introduced in New Zealand whereby the number of parliamentary seats for a political party was determined by its proportion of the total votes cast. Under this system the number of Maori seats, determined by the number of Maori registered on the Maori electoral roll, has increased to seven. Unfortunately for Maori voters, the total number of seats in Parliament has also increased to 120 and so indigenous influence remains relatively weak. Maori disillusionment with the ability of their MPs to represent their indigenous interests effectively in Parliament remains widespread, therefore, and some politicians are calling for the abolition of the Maori seats.

In my view, criticism of the indigenous seats is misdirected. Provided that the number of indigenous electorates is large enough to represent the

Maori population fully, this system ensures that there is indigenous influence within Parliament. Through this system indigenous people are able to participate in the political process as indigenous citizens and can be certain that their views will be articulated within Parliament. The problem is with the proviso – the full diversity of Maori opinion is not represented in the New Zealand system because only half of the Maori population votes in indigenous electorates. If all Maori registered to vote in Maori electorates the number of Maori seats would increase to around fourteen, greatly enhancing the ability of Maori to influence the legislative process. The problem, then, is not the system of indigenous seats but the ability of Maori to reject indigenous citizenship as expressed in their voting practices; the number of Maori who choose to participate in the political process as indigenous citizens is relatively small.

The pursuit of greater indigenous power through the ballot box has also been attempted in Latin America. Following the signing, by most Latin American countries, of the ILO Convention 169, indigenous rights have been included in the constitutions of Argentina, Bolivia, Colombia, Ecuador, Nicaragua, Panama, Paraguay, Peru and Venezuela. Most countries have now declared themselves to be pluri-ethnic and/or multicultural. The democratic challenge for indigenous leaders has been to transform words and ideals into new policies through greater participation in national politics. There have been some notable successes in countries where, like New Zealand, indigenous people make up a relatively large percentage of the population. In Ecuador, a mainly Indian political party, Pachakutik (meaning 'reawakening' in the Quechua language) now holds 19 out of 215 municipalities, 5 out of 22 provincial governorships and 10 per cent of the seats in Congress. In Bolivia, the mainly Indian Movement to Socialism and the local Pachakutik party polled almost a third of the vote in the last election. In Peru, where there are no significant indigenous parties, urban Quecha-speakers (known as *cholos*) are having an increasing impact on political life, especially as local mayors.

But, when indigenous citizenship is minority citizenship, no democracy based on majority voting can ever fully represent indigenous interests. Cultural nationalism and dreams of territorial separation are, therefore, understandable responses to majoritarian democracy. In Australia, for example, the voting power of Aboriginal people, who comprise a little over two per cent of the country's total population, is always going to be negligible unless new structures of representation are created. As I have already suggested, one possibility might be a variation on the Nunavut model. While Aboriginal people make up a small percentage of the country as a whole, in the Northern Territory they comprise almost 30 per cent of the population and there are large areas within this territory where they are the majority. But it is unlikely that a Nunavut-type model would significantly increase Aboriginal political influence within Australia. Its viability would depend upon a greatly increased willingness by the Australian government to recognize Aboriginal self-determination and this, in turn, would depend on a massive shift in public opinion.

Both territorial separation and cultural nationalism face enormous problems in gaining acceptance from post-settler majorities and will probably never be realistic possibilities for most indigenous minorities. Indigenous citizenship will find its fullest and most effective political expression in contexts where participatory – as opposed to formal – democracy has been developed to a very high level. In such circumstances formal democracy becomes a political shell protecting local and indigenous participation in decision-making in a wide range of organizations. Indigenous citizenship will underpin distinctive forms of political participation arising from particular relationships with the land and other property and the desire for indigenous languages and cultures to be maintained and developed. All citizens have an interest in ensuring diverse forms of political participation within a nation; political initiatives tied to an expansion of participatory democracy are likely to attract wider support than initiatives aimed at territorial or cultural partition.

# CHAPTER SIX

# Indigenous Recovery

On a windy afternoon in December 2003 I stood for four hours in a large tent as lawyers politely grilled me. I was presenting historical evidence to New Zealand's Waitangi Tribunal, which had convened in the small Maori settlement of Te Waimana to hear compensation claims relating to the loss of land and sovereignty. It was, for me, the culmination of years of research on the colonial history of the community, while for the mainly local audience seated in the tent it was a means of putting on public record truths that had been remembered for generations. I was anxious, since much depended on how well I and others presented our evidence. At stake was the extent to which the government would compensate the Tuhoe tribe for the following: the unjustified confiscation of their land, the imposition of a land court, the creation of a national park, and their loss of political independence.

When the cross-examination was over I left the tent, exhausted, and took a walk up the valley to the house where I had lived when carrying out my initial research. I was reminded of how successfully the Land Court had done its job. Where once hundreds of people had made a living through cash cropping and subsistence gardening, now just three families ran dairy farms on the land that remained in tribal hands. Most of the others in the community were either retired or unemployed. What would the outcome of the tribunal hearings mean for these people, I wondered? What would it mean for the hundreds, perhaps thousands, of others who have left for cities and jobs elsewhere? What could now be returned? What would it be used for? Who would it be returned to? Questions such as these were going through my head as I walked up the valley and they are at the forefront of my mind now as I consider broader questions of indigenous recovery.

If colonization was and is dispossession, then the futures of first peoples will be built on repossession. Indigenous cultures are not only cultures that were 'here first'; they are, as I have emphasized in this book, the colonized cultures of people who, in the process of colonization, have suffered enormous loss – the loss of children, the loss of land, the loss of authenticity, the loss of sovereignty. Indigenism is the taking back of these things, a reclaiming, not of past lives, but of the present conditions for future lives within post-settler states. The processes of colonial appropriation and indigenous repossession are always also transformations: what is appropriated is never the same as that which was lost, and in the process of reappropriation meaning and significance are further transformed. This is why I began this book with a brief account of the 'borrowing' and return of the Maori meeting-house named 'Mataatua'. It seemed to me that, in many ways, the history of Mataatua could serve as an allegory for the wider processes of colonial dispossession, indigenous repossession and the complex transformations in meaning and value that were inherent in both. In this final chapter, therefore, I want to return to Mataatua as a place from which to reflect more generally on relationships between indigenous loss, recovery and meaning.

In light of recent discussions around the notion of indigenous intellectual property, I think it is crucial to maintain a distinction between ownership and possession, and not to lose sight of the fact that, ultimately, the latter is most at stake. Indigenous ownership is about rights, today usually legal rights, whereas possession is the agency that these rights constrain or enable, authorize or prohibit. To say that I own something that you possess is not at all to specify what you may do with your possession. It may imply that you should give it back, but it may not. To ask, 'who owns native culture?', as one author has done recently in a book of this title,[1] is to pose a very different question about indigenous property from 'who possesses native culture?' I am here interested in issues surrounding the latter question only. The colonial appropriation of Mataatua for purposes of display was less a change of ownership than it was an act of dispossession, that is, it most crucially entailed the physical extraction of the building from a field of indigenous agency. While legal debates were clearly important in authorizing the recent restoration of the meeting-house to the field of indigenous agency, I do not discuss in any detail here legal issues surrounding indigenous property, intellectual or otherwise.

Mataatua was built as a political symbol by New Zealand's Ngati Awa tribe. It spoke most directly and powerfully, not to settlers, but to neighbouring tribes, Tuhoe and Te Whakatohea, who shared oral traditions about the arrival of their ancestors in a single canoe named Mataatua. In naming the house after the great ancestral vessel, Ngati Awa leaders were asserting a shared kinship and a common cause in opposition to settlers. They were also asserting their indigeneity. When I asked Tame Takao, an elder from Te Waimana, why traditions associated with Mataatua were significant for his Tuhoe people, he replied:

> It seems to me that what the Tuhoe people are trying to say is 'we have a right to be here, we have a right to the land here, here is our *whakapapa* [genealogy], here is our relationship to the land'. I think it's because of the frustration after the arrival of the Pakeha [settlers] with the gradual taking away of land, *mana* [ancestral power], religious beliefs and what it is to be Maori. That's why these things about . . . Mataatua came to the fore – to prove to

whoever is listening that, surely, the Maori should be part of the development and control of this country.[2]

The appropriation of Mataatua by the New Zealand government entailed the transformation of an indigenous symbol into a national one; rather than speaking to tribal leaders about indigenous unity and opposition to settlement it spoke, now, to others outside the country about New Zealand's 'primitive' past and 'civilized' future. In order that it might do so it was necessary that any voices that might suggest political agency in the indigenous present be silenced. Colonial dispossession – whether it was of children, land, authenticity or sovereignty – was always, more generally, a removal from indigenous agency and a silencing or marginalizing of the voices that animated that agency.

Children are not possessions in the same way that meeting-houses or land are. They are our kin, our 'blood', our future – or they are somebody else's. On my desk I have a photograph of my seven-year-old son, Hugo, in action mode on a beach – I think he was being Aragorn or Legolas from *Lord of the Rings*. It is very clear from the picture that we are dealing here with a strong-willed agent – he is challenging the viewer with a long driftwood stick, looking me in the eye. This child, like all children, discovers himself within a complex field of human agency – buildings and objects do not do this. The colonial dispossession of children was, therefore, as much a procedure of *making* possession as it was of taking possession. In removing children from their home communities, in severing their living ties with parents, siblings, grandparents and a world of other kin, colonial governments in Australia, the United States and Canada were making indigenous children into national property by depriving them and their parents of their cultural agency. As we have seen, this deprivation all too commonly took the form of abductions, incarcerations and brutal regimes of punishment. It would not be stretching the point too much to argue, therefore, that in the process of national appropriation indigenous children were, like Mataautua, turned inside out and given new pasts. Certainly boarding schools emptied or sought to empty children of their culture and language in order to fill them with new values and ways of being.

Although the national appropriation of children was only ever partially successful, in that many children and parents actively resisted assimilation through schooling, the children that indigenous communities now seek to 'repossess' are very different from those originally taken. Just as Mataatua returned was not Mataauta borrowed – some of its carvings and all of the latticework panels had been replaced – so too had indigenous children been 'reconstructed'. But repossession in both cases was less a recovery of the past than a return of things or people to indigenous agency. In the case of children, repossession has meant relocating schools within rural and urban fields of indigenous intent, both of which have changed radically since children were originally removed. Thus it is other children and new communities that are now being connected in projects of cultural renewal; if assimilation was separation, as I argued in chapter Four, then repossession is reconnection.

In chapter Four I further proposed that we should view assimilation as settlement, that the simultaneous dispossession of indigenous children and indigenous land were central to the settlement process. Like children, indigenous land had to undergo a process of cultural erasure and re-inscription before becoming national property. It had to be surveyed, mapped, blocked, subdivided, legally described, given a monetary value and fenced. Land that had not been subjected to these and other state-directed actions was considered to be outside the territory of the settler nation, on the other side of the frontier and in need of proper definition and administration.

Much of the legislation concerning indigenous land in settler states was directed at removing land from the control of traditional leaders, often by creating lists of individual owners for legally surveyed blocks. For example, the main objective of the New Zealand Native Land Court, established in 1865, was to replace collective kin-group ownership with titles derived from the Crown, thus enabling the government or private individuals to bypass kin-group leaders and deal directly with individual owners when acquiring land. Once government purchasers had accumulated enough shares in a block through dealing, sometimes in secret, with individuals they could apply to have their interests partitioned off, leaving those who had not agreed to sell with small, fragmented and uneconomic segments. In the end, the only rational course of action for many people was to sell these segments as well.

A parallel process occurred in the United States where reservation land was broken into allotments. Vine Deloria notes:

> Indian reservations with allotments have a multitude of problems that unallotted reservations do not have. It is exceedingly difficult to create economic grazing or farming units on allotted reservations because quite often there are not enough allotments contiguous to one another to make up an economically feasible block of land for leasing or tribal use . . . Land consolidation remains the major unsolved economic problem of Indian tribes.[3]

In Western Australia Aboriginal land became national land through the issuing of pastoral leases. The land of the Yawur people on the Roebuck Plains, north-west Australia, was assigned to a leaseholder with the following words:

> Elizabeth the Second, by the Grace of God, of the United Kingdom, Australia and her other Realms and Territories, Queen, Head of the Commonwealth, Defender of the Faith. To all whom these Presents shall come, Greeting: Know Ye that we of our especial Grace and in exercise of the powers in this behalf to Us given by the Land Act, 1933, and Amendments do by these presents

lease to . . . [proper name] . . . and assign the natural surface of all that parcel of land situated in the district of Dampier and containing 717,851 acres as delineated by a border of green colour on the plan herein . . . etc. etc.[4]

When the linguist and writer Stephen Muecke sought to travel across this land with Paddy Roe, a descendant of the Aboriginal owners, their way was blocked:

> If one wants to drive through the country one comes up against the barrier of the boundary fences which have gates with locks. These cut across the tracks Paddy Roe's people use to follow. Short of destroying these fences, the only way to gain access to the country is to drive to the homestead and ask the manager or owner for a key. We did this on several occasions, Paddy Roe bringing a diplomatic boomerang: a metaphorical key perhaps, one that would 'unlock' any opposition from the station people.[5]

The children who had been living on this land in the first decades of the twentieth century were sent to mission schools. Half-caste children like Paddy Roe were abducted and sent to Beagle Bay Mission, north of the Roebuck Plains. Paddy had escaped this fate only because his mother, on seeing the approaching police, had rolled him up in a blanket:

> P'lice was gonna pick me up – well err all the half-cast childrens you know p'lice pick-em-up whole lot – but my mother didn't want to let me go . . . 'come here boy' [s]he said – so [s]he put me there, 'lay down', rolled me up – wind me up an' mother was sitting on me like a swag here's a p'liceman coming around the corner now . . . [6]

When the land became leasehold property (in the name of the Queen) and the children mission property (in the name of the nation) it became impossible for men of Paddy Roe's father's generation to pass on to their children knowledge about the land or of the culture that was built on this knowledge. The loss of land and children meant also that the connections between them became more *ad hoc* and tenuous, if they were made at all.

Much of the land that is now being reclaimed and repossessed by indigenous peoples has, in the period between dispossession and reappropriation, become a commodity; it has been surveyed, 'opened up', fenced, built upon and sold. Moreover, although the land is, in most cases, being returned to the descendants of those who formerly possessed it, their kingroups have been radically transformed, in large part as a result of the original alienation. What does repossession mean for the Oneida Indians, for example, who lost more than two hundred thousand acres in central New York, or the tribes of Wellington, New Zealand, who lost thousands of acres and access to the sea when New Zealand's capital city was founded and developed? These claims and hundreds of others like them cannot possibly be settled by a simple return of the land that was lost. Instead, the original fraud or treaty breach has to be recognized and addressed through settlement packages that include a mixture of land, money and other forms of compensation – in the case of the Oneida Indians, gambling rights and an off-reservation casino were on offer in addition to land and millions of dollars. Indigenous repossession is, therefore, frequently synonymous with capitalist development and the growth of tribal corporations. This is so, irrespective of whether urban or rural land is at issue. Even when rural land is returned it often becomes a resource for tourist ventures, forestry or other capitalist enterprises. In some cases, the profits from such developments are being ploughed back into indigenous education, the repossession of children.

The dispossession of indigenous identity appears, on the surface, to be quite a different process from the taking of meeting-houses, children or land. Most obviously, the latter have material existences whereas identity exists mainly in the realm of ideas. But the taking or removing of indigenous objects or persons and the taking of indigenous ideas are fundamentally the same in one crucial respect – all are a transference of possessions of value from fields of indigenous agency to fields of settler agency. In the case of identity, indigenous self-definition became subject to the discursive constraints of colonial representation, especially those that we now associate with the discourse of primitivism. Like Edward Said's 'Orientalism', primitivism was a production of generalizing and authoritative 'truths' about others subjected to western rule. It supplied the ruled with certain mentalities, personalities and essential natures. Just as Orientalism as a discursive field *produced* the Oriental, so primitivism *produced* the primitive as a person who might be knowledgeably governed.

Summarizing the systematic, controlling power of Orientalism, Said wrote:

> So authoritative a position did Orientalism have, that I believe no one writing, thinking or acting on the Orient could do so without taking account of the limitations of thought and action imposed by Orientalism. In brief, because of Orientalism the Orient was not (and is not) a free subject of thought and action.[7]

Forced to speak from within a discursive field that defined their voices as those of the past, indigenous leaders were as constrained as anyone speaking or writing on the Orient. But primitivism within settler states differed from Orientalism in one critical respect: it was more closely tied to evolutionary narratives that temporalized and legitimized settler nations. By locating all indigenous knowledge, including self-knowledge, at an evolutionary level below that of settlers, primitivist discourse defined this knowledge and identity as the potential property of those best able to preserve it. It licensed a veritable industry of salvage ethnography staffed, in the main, by settlers, who, believing that they were preserving 'tribal' identities, were in truth participating in their production.

It was not only the generalizing and essentializing discourse of primitivism that constrained the ability of indigenous people to control their identity; the particularizing discourses of official tribalism and blood quantum were equally oppressive in depriving people of the ability to create 'authentic' self-identities. We saw, in chapter Two, that official tribalism can act as an exclusionary discourse in countries, such as New Zealand, where the majority of the indigenous people are urban and where many do not know their genealogies. There is no need for me to elaborate further here on the absurdities of blood politics in the United States. In both cases, particular indigenous identities became matters of state definition; authentic indigeneity became a government grant, able to be given to and withdrawn from particular people in particular circumstances.

It goes without saying that the identities over which indigenous people now seek control are not those that were lost. What is being reclaimed is the ability to be diversely authentic in a rejection of the racism and essentialism that characterized settler regimes of identification. Peoples are insisting that they be known by their particular tribal names, rather than as 'Indians', 'Aborigines' or 'Maori', and that the spelling of these names is correct. Aboriginal people in south-east Australia have, for example, rejected the generalizing label in favour of their own name – Koori. Prior to the 1960s other names such as 'coorie' and 'kooli', which all meant 'person' or 'people', were in use but the spelling and pronunciation has since been standardized as Koori. A similar process has occurred throughout Australia so that now, in south and central Queensland, the name 'Murra' is preferred, while 'Nyoongah' is the term of self-identification around Perth in Western Australia.

In contrast to this particularizing of identity in Australia, peoples of Canada's West Coast living around Port Rupert insist upon a more generalized identity. Partly as a result of numerous anthropological publications about the Kwakiutl, this name came to be extended to a number of different neighbouring tribes. These tribes and the Kwakiutl now prefer to identify themselves as members of the larger Kwakwaka'wakw nation. In New Zealand the general name 'Maori' was first used by Maori people themselves in the nineteenth century, while settlers more commonly used the term 'Native'. Although 'Maori' remains in common use by Maori nationalists, tribal or *iwi* names are increasingly preferred. Thus both generalized and particularized identities are here being developed simultaneously. Whatever the preferred name, however, the right to name is now unquestionably an indigenous one.

But the repossession of indigenous identity is more than reclaiming the right to self-naming. It is also, as I noted in chapter Two, about expanding the definition of what counts as indigenous in fields such as art and music. How strong do 'traditional' influences have to be in a contemporary work of art for it to be considered indigenous? Do there need to be any traditional influences at all? Is it simply the message or significance that defines a work as indigenous? Is it merely the fact that the artist identifies as indigenous? By raising questions of this sort about indigenous art, artists such as Jimmie Durham opened up broader ones that relate to the field of indigenous identity in general. And they are not the sorts of questions with which post-settler governments are comfortable, because they have no definitive answers.

The dispossession of indigenous children, land and identity was ultimately enabled by the more general dispossession of indigenous sovereignty. The dispossession of indigenous sovereignty was understood by settler governments to be the possession, by them and their settler nations, of entire indigenous populations. This was reflected in official and popular publications that asked what should be done about 'our Aborigines', 'our Maoris' or 'our Indians'. Such writings were especially prevalent in the late nineteenth century in Canada, the United States, Australia and New Zealand, reflecting a widespread belief that if native peoples could not be saved from extinction they deserved to be better cared for in the meantime. Lady Mary Martin argued as much in 1884 in her book *Our Maoris*[8] and similar expressions of concern accompanied the passing of the Dawes Act in the United States. In Australia, the government could still produce publications with titles such as *The Skills of Our Aborigines*[9] in 1967, while Indians in Brazil are still officially regarded as national possessions – a recent art exhibition held at the Brazilian Embassy in Helsinki, opened to coincide with Brazilian Independence Day, was titled *Brazil, Our Indians, Our Art.*[10]

In the early twentieth century the government of British Columbia in Canada included in its *Yearbook* a section titled, 'Our Indians'. Under the subheading 'Their Place in the Nation', it was made clear, in 1901, that Indians were, like foster children and the mentally ill, wards of the Government – that the Canadian government was their guardian. But it is also apparent that this government 'care' required a centralized hierarchy of control and surveillance.

> The Indians of Canada are wards of the Dominion Government, which has an Indian Department especially organized to guard their interests and to attend to their requirements. The Department is under the general superintendence of one of the Dominion Ministers of state, usually that of the Minister of the Interior. There is a Deputy Superintendent General of Indian Affairs under the supervision of the Minister who has immediate control of, and takes action in, all matters concerning the Indians and their general welfare. Connected with this Department there is in each Province of the Dominion of Canada a Superintendent of Indian Affairs who reports to the Deputy Superintendent General and receives his instructions. He is assisted by Indian Agents, clerks and other functionaries sufficient to carry out the object of Government.[11]

It was this pervasive control and surveillance, under the names of 'care' and 'improvement', that the dispossession of indigenous sovereignty meant in practice within all settler states. Paternalism was more than self-delusion on the part of settler governments; it became an authoritative discourse, spoken by colonizer and colonized because it expressed a real appropriation of indigenous sovereignty in the language of parental care and concern.

The dispossession of indigenous sovereignty entailed, in most cases, radical changes to the political life of indigenous communities through both the imposition of colonial rule and mobilization of resistance to it. It goes without saying, therefore, that the power that was lost is not the power that is being returned. The power that was lost was typically fully independent and religiously or ancestrally derived, whereas that which is returned is ultimately state-derived and managerial. The repossession of self-determination always assumes a new 'self' and a new mode of 'deter-mination'. The paradoxical question facing indigenous communities and post-settler states is, therefore: to which new selves should this new power be returned?

The assumption under which most post-settler states are operating is that power should be returned to communities that most resemble the ones who lost it. The leaders of these communities – and of course they are invariably rural – are thought to be able to establish the clearest lines of succession from the original people colonized. The difficulty is that there are now multiple lines of succession from those who were originally dispos-sessed and these extend to urban as well as rural people in the present. I noted in the previous chapter the limited ability of territorial sovereignty to address issues of indigenous self-determination and my point here is simply an extension of this argument. Many national and urban organiza-tions that often look quite unlike 'traditional' ones, but which legitimately represent indigenous interests, have a strong case for shares in the self-determination being returned by settler states.

Conceiving of indigenous politics as repossession raises the possibility that, as this process approaches a pragmatic or agreed end-point, indigeneity may begin to lose its political significance. As tribes become capitalist corporations, for example, dealing with post-settler states from positions of increased economic and political strength, will indigeneity be rejected as a label too closely associated with a former position of relative weakness? Will post-recovery mean post-indigenism, or will indigeneity endure well beyond the politics of grievance and redress?

Ngai Tahu, the main tribe in the South Island of New Zealand, may be on its way to becoming post-indigenous – certainly this is the future that some of its leaders envisage for themselves. Ngai Tahu is a tribe of about 33,000 signed-up members, many of whom live outside their tribal territory in New Zealand and Australian cities. Following a protracted settlement process, the New Zealand government formally apologized to the tribe for treaty breaches and paid $170 million in compensation to it. This money has since been invested in tourism, property, seafood businesses and shares, and its total assets are now almost $400 million. As the tribe becomes a larger player in the local economy some of the leaders no longer want to be regarded as indigenous. As one leader put it, 'liberals still see Maori as an indigenous person who needs to be saved by historic restitution of their old claims'.[12] He and others in the tribe now find that liberalism has become a hindrance to their pursuit of profit; rather than being regarded as indigenous they prefer to be dealt with as significant property owners.

Maintaining linkages between the tribe's urban-based leaders and its eighteen rural communities is important for decision making and the distribution of wealth, but Ngai Tahu do not want their children to be confined to such communities. An educational unit prepares secondary school children for tertiary education and establishes partnerships between the tribe and national tertiary institutions. Children are given every opportunity to learn Maori, but they are also expected to become multilingual by taking Asian and European languages at school. It is intended that these 'post-indigenous' children will know their heritage but also be able to pursue successful careers in national and global market-places. The tribe has entered into business partnerships with international companies and aims to become a global corporate over the next 50 years. It is expected that the tribe's 'post-indigenous' children will participate in this embrace of global capitalism and become 'post-indigenous' citizens whose interests will reflect their cosmopolitanism as much as their tribal identity.

Such views are, however, by no means mainstream within New Zealand, and cultural nationalists in New Zealand, Hawai'i, Canada, the United States and Latin America have vigorously denounced this tribal capitalism and its right-leaning ideology. Market forces and individualism, it is argued, are the very antithesis of fundamental indigenous values such as cooperation and kin-group belonging. However, when relatively large sums of money are transferred from states to indigenous corporations their leaders have few options but to invest the money in profit-making ventures. When the growth of large investments is at stake the interests of tribal corporations tend to become allied with those of other large business operations. Post-indigenism can appear to be an entirely reasonable vision for some managers operating in these circumstances. But for the many millions of indigenous people who have not received large compensation payments or who are unlikely to receive any tangible 'trickle-down' benefits in the foreseeable future, this corporate post-indigenism has little resonance.

The main weakness inherent in the above concept of 'post-indigenism' is, however, that it envisages changes to indigenous identities within existing post-settler nations rather than identifying more radical transformations of post-settler nationhood itself. The notion of a post-indigenous identity too easily affirms old narratives of nationhood that have progressive 'settlement' as their master trope. These narratives have been rewritten during the process of indigenous repossession over the last twenty years or so, replacing 'settlement' with 'dialogue' or 'engagement'. Partly as a result of this rewriting, we are now able to understand indigenous repossession as something more than assimilation by other means and to recognize indigeneity as an enduring condition at the heart of post-settler state legitimacy. Post-indigenism is simply old thinking dressed up as new.

I think indigenous repossession is better understood, not as a prelude to post-indigenism, but as an initial stage in a longer process of post-colonialism. Yes, I know post-colonialism is a very slippery and widely disputed concept. It has been criticized for its over-simplistic periodization – a binary distinction between 'then' and 'now' – and its over-generalized scope, lumping together Third World diasporas with indigenous politics.[13] It has been argued that, rather than a description of anything, 'post-colonialism' is simply a discourse that seeks to define the world from the position of diasporic, Third World intellectuals, thus concealing profound continuities in the spread of global capitalism. But I am attracted to Stuart Hall's defence of the term. He argues that post-colonialism is a *process* that involves the disengagement of colonizers and colonized from their former relationships of mutual entanglement and definition. It is, he suggests, 'A general process of decolonization which, like colonization itself, has marked the colonizing societies as powerfully as it has the colonized (of course in different ways).'[14] In other words, post-colonialism is a condition of both post-settler nations and indigenous peoples as they seek to redefine the terms of their relationship with each other. Understood from this post-colonial perspective, indigenous repossession is a necessary initial stage in a longer process that will ultimately result in new forms of indigenous belonging within post-settler nations and new locations for indigenous people within these imagined communities.

In his insightful analysis of the United States Indian struggle, *Nations Within*, Vine Deloria distinguished between 'tribal Indians' and 'ethnic Indians'. The struggle for nationhood by tribal Indians 'imagines a time when each tribe will have some kind of parity with other nations of the world, as each tribe believes it had prior to contact with Europeans'. The concerns of ethnic Indians arise from experiences of urban injustice, racism and inequality. They tend to regard tribal people as 'overly romantic' and as 'putting too much trust in the ability of American Institutions to perform moral acts that would be necessary to secure what they want'. At the forefront of the Indian movement in the 1970s, ethnic Indians sought new forms of political participation that extended beyond the reservation and formal federal-tribal relations.[15]

I think that we can usefully generalize Deloria's distinction in order to conceptualize contemporary post-colonial formations within post-settler states as being founded on a three-way relationship between tribally indigenous, ethnically indigenous and non-indigenous:

## The Post-colonial Field (very simplified)

Tribally Indigenous            Ethnically Indigenous

Non-indigenous

Rather than a binary relationship between colonizer and colonized, the growing political significance of urban indigeneity means that there are now complex renegotiations occurring simultaneously on three levels, with each level affecting the others. Alternatively, we might view the post-colonial field as consisting of three binary relationships, each of which is disrupted or interrupted by a third voice: relations between tribally indigenous and ethnically indigenous peoples are mediated by the relationships that each has with post-settler states, the latter representing non-indigenous interests; negotiations between post-settler states and tribally indigenous people are always within hearing of ethnically indigenous people, and the voices of the latter cannot be ignored by either party; finally, inter-ethnic relations between ethnically indigenous people and non-indigenous people within multicultural contexts are always against a background of assumed tribal authenticity and tribal-state relations centred upon land.

None of the three categories within the post-colonial field is likely to disappear, as might be envisaged in the notion of post-indigenism: tribal indigeneity is being strengthened by the repossession processes that we have just been considering, ethnic indigeneity is being strengthened by urbanization and non-indigeneity persists in contrast with the other two. Moreover, membership in any one of the three categories is not static, shifting over time and across generations – identification with tribes has, in some cases, increased as assets have been returned to them, but this movement from ethnic to tribal is matched by identity shifts in the other direction as people's life-circumstances change through urbanization, intermarriage, occupational mobility and the effects of state policy. There is also a continuous shuffling of people between the categories of indigenous and non-indigenous: in Canada and Australia there have, over the last twenty years or so, been large increases in the percentages of people self-identifying themselves as indigenous in the national census and there have been lesser increases elsewhere. And, of course, there are always flows in the opposite direction.

The non-indigenous category has a very diverse membership, including post-settler majorities as well as numerous migrant and diasporic minorities. The ethnic politics internal to this category is generally described as multicultural, although the meaning of this term differs greatly between post-settler states. North American multiculturalism, for example, is usually about the place of migrant minorities within the post-settler nation, whereas Latin American multiculturalism is usually about enabling greater indigenous participation in democracy. Indigenous peoples in North America (and also in Australia and New Zealand) quite reasonably fear that their distinctive relations with the state will be framed in terms of an official multiculturalism that denies their primacy, but such concerns are largely absent in South America where multiculturalism ideally affirms indigenous rights. In New Zealand, multiculturalism is sometimes described as extending a more fundamental bicultural relationship that opposes the category of indigenous to all other ethnic categories. While there is official support for Maori insistence that multiculturalism be founded upon biculturalism, this is also an increasingly contested claim.

Indigenous repossession has been, up until now, a tribally centred process though which control over land, education and other social services has been transferred from states to indigenous territorial administrations. Indigenous ethnic organizations have been funded to provide social services, including education, for indigenous people in urban areas and they have been included in settlement deals between governments and tribes, but their participation in the recovery and repossession process has generally been of a marginal nature. The distribution, between ethnically and tribally indigenous people, of the assets that have been recovered is already a significant issue in many post-settler states and it is likely to increase in significance as the value of tribal assets increases.

The dispute, discussed in chapter Two, between urban Maori organizations and Maori tribes over the allocation of fish quota may herald others that are more crucially about the nature of self-determination and locus of indigenous power in New Zealand. The ways in which indigenous self-determination might be shared between urban off-reserve people and their 'home' communities has already become a vital issue in Canada, especially in British Columbia, where 70 per cent of Aboriginal people reside off reserve. Not all of these off-reserve people have severed their ties with reserves – many are urban and tribal – but increasing numbers prefer more generalized ethnic identities.

A number of different models have recently been proposed to address the tragic failure to distribute power and resources fairly between reserve and off-reserve people in Canada. One suggestion is that the governance of reserve-based nations be extended to members living in cities and that off-reserve people have voting rights in elections of Indian Band Councils. These rights have been recently affirmed in a Canadian Supreme Court decision that struck down the reserve residency requirements of the Indian

Act. But this model leaves many tricky issues unresolved. Because the Aboriginal populations of cities like Vancouver have very diverse origins, the coordination of urban services provided by numerous reserve-based administrations would be extremely difficult. Achieving equality of access to services for all Aboriginal peoples would be almost impossible given different levels of resources available to reserve governments. Alternative models propose that urban Aboriginal communities be given a measure of self-governance independently of reserve-based structures. These too face enormous difficulties, not the least of which is that they leave the political and economic relationships between urban and reserve-based administrations unresolved.

New linkages between urban, ethnically indigenous people and rural land-based communities are needed, not only to facilitate more equitable distributions of power and resources, but also to create stronger collective voices in relation to post-settler governments. The rural–urban political divide has been bridged periodically during major demonstrations and marches in support of land rights and autonomy, but there is everywhere a need for more enduring structures. Recently, on the edge of Mexico City, Nahuatl Indians, who claim descent from Aztec ancestors, have aligned themselves with rural Zapatistas in their efforts to achieve greater political autonomy for their communities. They do so at a time when the urbanization of indigenous people is increasing dramatically – I noted earlier that around 40 per cent of Mexico's indigenous people are now urban, many forced to leave their villages by the fall in corn prices that followed the implementation of the North American Free Trade Agreement. In Mexico City the indigenous population has, since 1990, quadrupled to about half a million. Yet, although they frequently invoke the name 'Zapatista', most urban communities have no formal political links with those leading the rural struggle. Such links are urgently needed, not only in Mexico, but also in all post-settler states if the divisive politics of authenticity is to be contested successfully.

Whereas post-indigenism envisages an end-point in the struggles of indigenous peoples to recover what was lost through colonialism, post-colonialism, as I have defined it, envisages ongoing and changing relationships between tribally indigenous, ethnically indigenous and non-indigenous people. First peoples are becoming more culturally diverse, but they are becoming more culturally diverse in indigenous ways and the future politics of indigeneity will undoubtedly reflect this fact. Indigenous cultures today are neither rural nor urban but an articulation – a connecting up – of both in the back and forth shuttling of everyday life. To seek the true centres of indigenous cultures in rural subsistence communities or to become excited about a future of urban hybridity is to miss what is happening in between. Here, parents and grandparents are sharing food and memories with children and grandchildren who have returned 'home' for the school holidays, city artists and writers are drawing upon rural imagery and ancient legends to give themselves an edge in the national market-place, and urban leaders are criticizing the conservatism of tribal leaders while the latter struggle to justify their positions. These are the sorts of enduring relations through which both tribal and ethnic identities persist and change. One can hardly imagine how they will be interacting in 50, 100 or 500 years.

But, difficult though it may be, we have to start actively imagining such indigenous futures: nobody can assume any more that first peoples will not be around in 500 years time. Whether or not their cultures become more secure sources of identity within post-colonial nations is another matter. For this to happen, post-settler governments will need to abandon the politics of oppressive authenticity and accept that indigenous identity is multiple and on the move. They will need to engage politically with a broader spectrum of indigenous peoples than they do now and include a greater diversity of indigenous futures in their narratives of post-colonial nationhood. And it goes without saying that, in doing this, post-settler governments would be wise to take their lead from first peoples.

# References

## Chapter One: Indigenism

1 Nicholas Thomas, *Possessions: Indigenous Art/Colonial Culture* (London, 1999), p. 109.

2 Ngati Awa Trust Board, 'The Meetinghouse Mataatua: Summary Paper' (n.d.).

3 Marshall Sahlins, 'What is Anthropological Enlightenment? Some Lessons of the Twentieth Century', *Annual Review of Anthropology*, XXVIII (1999), p. 7.

4 Ian McIntosh, 'UN Permanent Forum on Indigenous Issues', *Anthropology Today*, XVII/6 (2001), p. 23.

5 Quoted by Douglas Sanders, 'Background Information on the Formation of the World Council of Indigenous Peoples', MS from Centre for World Indigenous Studies, New York, 1980, p. 3.

6 Ibid., p. 4.

7 Ibid., p. 7.

8 Andrea Muehlebach, '"Making Place" at the United Nations: Indigenous Cultural Politics at the UN Working Group on Indigenous Populations', *Cultural Anthropology*, XVI/3 (2001), p. 420.

9 Ibid., p. 436.

10   Ibid., p. 423; Pramod Parajuli, 'Rethinking Ethnicity: Developmentalist Hegemonies and Emergent Identities in India', *Identities: Global Studies in Culture and Power*, III (1996), pp. 15–59.

11   *Fourth World Bulletin* (July 1994), Commentary, p. 1; Patrick Thornberry, p. 376.

12   Alcida Rita Ramos, *Indigenism: Ethnic Politics in Brazil* (Madison, WI, 1998), p. 7.

13   Apirana Ngata to Te Rangi Hiroa, in M.P.K. Sorrenson, ed., *Na to Hoa Aroha, from Your Dear Friend: The Correspondence of Sir Apirana Ngata and Sir Peter Buck, 1925–50* (Auckland, 1986–8)

## Chapter Two: Oppressive Authenticity

1   Alcida Rita Ramos, *Indigenism: Ethnic Politics in Brazil* (Madison, WI, 1998), pp. 84–5.

2   Mary Douglas, *Purity and Danger: An Analysis of the Concepts of Pollution and Taboo* (London, 1966), pp. 51, 71.

3   Patrick Wolfe, 'Nation and Miscegenation: Discursive Continuity in the post-Mabo Era', *Social Analysis*, XXXVI (1994), p. 110.

4   Cited by Beth Conklin, 'Body Paint, Feathers and VCRs: Aesthetics and Authenticity in Amazonian Activism', *American Anthropologist*, XXIV (1997), p. 714.

5   Ibid., p. 721.

6   Ibid., p. 727.

7   Peter Read, *The Stolen Generations: The Removal of Aboriginal Children in NSW 1883 to 1969* (NSW Dept of Aboriginal Affairs, 1998).

8   Wolfe, 'Nation and Miscegenation', p. 114.

9   Ibid., p. 116.

10   *Bringing Them Home: Report of the National Inquiry into the Separation of Aboriginal and Torres Strait Islander Children from their Families*

(Canberra, 1997).

11  The first member of the stolen generations to win compensation was awarded $35,000 by the New South Wales Compensation Tribunal in October 2002.

12  D'Arcy McNickle, *Native American Tribalism: Indian Survivals and Renewals* (Oxford, 1973), pp. 82–3.

13  Ibid., pp. 83–4.

14  Circe Sturm, *Blood Politics: Race, Culture and Identity in the Cherokee Nation of Oklahoma* (London, 2002), p. 78.

15  Ibid., pp. 2–3.

16  Ibid., p. 97.

17  Ibid., p. 208.

18  Ibid., p. 100.

19  Laura Turney, 'Ceci n'est pas Jimmie Durham', *Critique of Anthropology*, XIX (1999).

20  Ibid., p. 430.

21  Ibid., p. 436.

22  Harry Daniels, 'Bill C-31: The Abocide Bill: Overview of Bill C-31', www.abo-peoples.org/programs/C-31/Abocide/Abocide-2.html

23  Mason Durie, *Te Mana, Te Kawanatanga: The Politics of Maori Self-determination* (Auckland, 1998), p. 228.

24  Julie Gough, 'History, Representation, Globalisation and Indigenous Cultures: A Tasmanian Perspective', in *Indigenous Cultures in an Interconnected World*, ed. C. Smith and G. Ward (St Leonards, NSW, 2000), p. 92.


## Chapter Three: Urban Indigeneity


1  Phillip Wearne, *The Return of the Indian: Conquest and Revival in the Americas* (London, 1996), p. 150.

2  Kerry Buchanan, 'A Maori Warrior Claims New Territory', *The Courier*, July–August 2000.

3  Cited in Davianna McGregor, 'Ho'omauke ea o ka Lahui Hawai'i: The Perpetuation of the Hawai'ian People', in *Ethnicity and Nation-building in the South Pacific*, ed. M. Howard (UNESCO, 1989), pp. 92–3.

4  Wearne, *Return of the Indian*, pp. 173–4.

5  Ibid., p. 175.

6  'Commonly Asked Questions about Ka Lahui Hawai'i', www.cwis.org/fwdp/oceania/hawaiques.txt.

## Chapter Four: Indigenous Children

1  Theresa McCarty, *A Place to be Navajo: Rough Rock and the Struggle for Self-determination in Indigenous Schooling* (Mahwah, NJ, 2002), p. 40.

2  New Zealand Government, *Appendices to the Journals of the House of Representatives*, 1934, G-11, pp. 46–7.

3  Deborah Bird Rose, *Hidden Histories: Black Stories from Victoria River Downs, Humber River and Wave Hill Stations* (Canberra, 1991), p. 46.

4  Quoted in R. Harker and K. McConnochie, *Education as Cultural Artifact: Studies in Maori and Aboriginal Education* (Palmerston North, 1985), p. 98.

5  Quentin Beresford, '"The Kids Get Lost": Confronting the Underlying Causes of Educational Disadvantage among Urban Aboriginal Children in Western Australia', *Indigenous Issues and the New Millennium*, Social Education Association of Australia Monograph (1998), p. 8.

6  Ibid.

7  McCarty, *A Place to be Navajo*, pp. 42–3.

8  Richard Perry, *From Time Immemorial: Indigenous Peoples and State*

*Systems* (Austin, TX, 1996), p. 141.

9 Judith Simon and Linda Tuhiwai Smith, eds, *A Civilising Mission? Perceptions and Representations of the New Zealand Native Schools System* (Auckland, 2001), p. 172.

10 Thomas Benjamin, 'A Time of Reconquest: History, the Maya Revival, and the Zapatista Rebellion in Chiapas', *American Historical Review*, CV (2000), pp. 417–50.

11 Ibid., p. 432.

12 Gabriela Vargas-Certina, 'Uniting in Difference: The Movement for a New Indigenous Education in the State of Chiapas, Mexico', *Urban Anthropology*, xxvii (1998), pp. 135–64.

13 Larry Miller, 'Our Communities are very Poor . . .', *Rethinking Schools*, XIV (1999), p. 2.

14 Harker and McConnochie, *Education as Cultural Artifact*.

15 Deirdre Jordan, 'Australian Aborigines: Education and Identity', in *Education and Cultural Differences: New Perspectives*, ed. Douglas Ray and Deo Poonwassie (New York), pp. 61–87.

16 McCarty, *A Place to be Navajo*, p. 199.

## Chapter Five: Indigenous Citizens

1 *Dominion Saturday Post*, 17 January 2004, p. E1.

2 Ibid.

3 Alcida Rita Ramos, *Indigenism: Ethnic Politics in Brazil* (Madison, WI, 1998), p. 94

4 Ibid., p. 247.

5 *Dominion Post*, 29 January 2004, p. B5.

6 Robert Porter, 'The Demise of the Ongwehoweh and the Rise of the Native Americans: Redressing the Genocidal Act of Forcing American

Citizenship upon Indigenous Peoples', *Harvard Blackletter Law Journal*, xv (1999), pp. 107–83.

7 Taiaiake Alfred, 'From Sovereignty to Freedom: Towards an Indigenous Political Discourse', *Indigenous Affairs* (2001), no. 3, p. 28.

8 Ibid., p. 34.

9 Speech delivered at a meeting between Cape York leaders and John Howard, 10 August 2003.

10 John Richards, 'Reserves Are Only Good for Some People', *Journal of Canadian Studies*, xxxv (2000), p. 197.

11 *Cultural Survival Quarterly* (Spring 1999), pp. 33–4.

## Chapter Six: Indigenous Recovery

1 Michael Brown, *Who Owns Native Culture?* (New York, 2004).

2 Jeffrey Sissons, *Te Waimana, the Spring of Mana: Tuhoe History and the Colonial Encounter* (Dunedin, 1991), p. 57.

3 Vine Deloria and Clifford Lytle, *The Nations Within: The Past and Future of American Indian Sovereignty* (Austin, TX, 1998), pp. 256–7.

4 Kim Benterrak, Steven Muecke and Paddy Roe, *Reading the Country* (Fremantle, 1984), p. 130.

5 Ibid., p. 66.

6 Ibid., p. 40.

7 Edward Said, *Orientalism* (London, 1978), p. 3.

8 Lady Mary Martin, *Our Maoris* (Auckland, 1884).

9 *The Skills of Our Aborigines*, Government Printer (Canberra, 1967).

10 www.brazil.fi/home.

11 Government of Canada, *Year Book of British Columbia* (Toronto, 1901), chapter 6, section 4.

12 Bruce Ansley, 'A Wealth of Talent', *New Zealand Listener* (6 March 2004), pp. 16–18.

13  Ella Shohat, 'Notes on the Postcolonial', *Social Text*, XXXI/XXXII (1992), pp. 99–113.
14  Stuart Hall, 'When Was the Post-colonial? Thinking at the Limit', in *The Post-Colonial Question: Common Skies, Divided Horizons*, ed. I. Chambers and L. Curti (London, 1996), p. 250.
15  Deloria and Lytle, *The Nations Within*, pp. 242–3.

# Select Bibliography

Brown, Michael, *Who Owns Native Culture?* (New York, 2004)

Deloria, Vine, and Clifford Lytle, *The Nations Within: The Past and Future of American Indian Sovereignty* (Austin, TX, 1998)

Durie, Mason, *Te Mana, Te Kawanatanga: The Politics of Maori Self-determination* (Auckland, 1998)

Fleras, Augie, and Jean Elliott, *The Nations Within: Aboriginal–State Relations in Canada, the United States and New Zealand* (Toronto, 1996)

Harvey, Neil, *The Chiapas Rebellion: The Struggle for Land and Democracy* (Durham, NC, 1998)

Ivison, Duncan, Paul Palton and Will Sanders, eds, *Political Theory and the Rights of Indigenous Peoples* (Melbourne, 2000)

McCarty, Theresa, *A Place to be Navajo: Rough Rock and the Struggle for Self-determination in Indigenous Schooling* (Mahwah, NJ, 2002)

Maybury-Lewis, David, *Indigenous Peoples, Ethnic Groups and the State* (Needham Heights, MA, 1997)

Niezen, Ronald, *The Origins of Indigenism: Human Rights and the Politics of Identity* (Berkeley, CA, 2003)

Perry, Richard, *From Time Immemorial: Indigenous Peoples and State Systems* (Austin, TX, 1996)

Povinelli, Elizabeth A., *The Cunning of Recognition: Indigenous Alterities and the Making of Australian Multiculturalism* (Durham, NC, 2002)

Ramos, Alcida Rita, *Indigenism: Ethnic Politics in Brazil* (Madison, WI, 1998)

Reynolds, Henry, *Aboriginal Sovereignty: Reflections on Race, State and Nation* (St Leonards, NSW, 1996)

Sieder, Rachel, ed., *Multiculturalism in Latin America: Indigenous Rights, Diversity and Democracy* (London, 2002)

Sturm, Circe, *Blood Politics: Race, Culture and Identity in the Cherokee Nation of Oklahoma* (London, 2002)

Thomas, Nicholas, *Possessions: Indigenous Art/Colonial Culture* (London, 1999)

Warren, Kay, *Indigenous Movements and their Critics: Pan-Maya Activism in Guatemala* (Princeton, NJ, 1998)

Wearne, Phillip, *The Return of the Indian: Conquest and Revival in the Americas* (London, 1996)

# Acknowledgements

My understanding of the lived realities of colonialism and indigenous identity has been developed and deepened through dialogue with the people of Te Waimana. I thank them for their patience and generosity. In particular I thank Tame Takao, who has never been afraid to confront difficult issues. Nicholas Thomas has supported this project from the beginning and I am very grateful for his helpful criticisms of my manuscript. Finally, I thank my family, Catherine, Isobel and Hugo, who have been a source of warmth through a very long Wellington winter.

# List of Illustrations

p. 6: A carved ancestral face at the apex of Mataatua, a New Zealand Maori meeting-house. The double tongue symbolizes dialogue between tribes. Photo reproduced courtesy of the Polynesian Society.

p. 36: A Nunivak ceremonial mask, Alaska, photographed by Edward S. Curtis in 1929. Photo: Library of Congress Prints and Photographs Division (Edward S. Curtis Collection; LC-USZ62-66041).

p. 60: Signs at the landing dock, Alcatraz, San Francisco Bay, welcoming Indian people to join the Native American occupation of the island, 1969-71. Photo: Michelle Vignes, courtesy of the Bancroft Library, University of California, Berkeley.

p. 84: Native American children in a mathematics class at Carlisle Indian School, Pennsylvania, photographed by Frances Benjamin Johnston *c.* 1903. Photo: Library of Congress (Frances Benjamin Johnston Collection; LC-USZ62-72450).

p. 112: The Australian Aboriginal tent embassy outside Parliament House, Canberra, 1972. Photo: National Archives of Australia (Department of Interior Series; image no. A7973 INT 1205/1).

p. 138: The Maori meeting-house, Mataatua, reassembled with the walls turned inside out at the Sydney Exhibition, 1880. Photo reproduced courtesy of the Polynesian Society.